The Wonderfvll

in the Covnrie ot Lancaster

The
Wonderfvll Discoverie
of Witches in the Covntie of Lancaster

Thomas Potts

Published by Carnegie Publishing Ltd
Carnegie House
Chatsworth Road
Lancaster
LA1 4SL

www.carnegiepublishing.com

British Library Cataloguing-in-Publication data
A CIP record for this book is available from the British Library

ISBN 1-85936-100-5

Typeset by Carnegie Publishing
Printed and bound in the UK by Biddles Ltd (Guildford)

Preface

THOMAS POTTS' BOOK is unique in that it is the only surviving contemporaneous account of a seventeenth-century trial before the invention of shorthand. It contains verbatim many of the examinations of witnesses upon which the trial was based. It was clearly published in order to curry favour with the judges to whom he had acted as clerk in the Lent and Summer Assizes of the Northern Circuit in 1612, and probably also to attempt to bring his work to the attention of King James I, who was one of the seventeenth-century authorities on witchcraft, and himself the author of one of the leading authorities – *Demonologie*, published in 1597, before he came to the English throne. (In contrast, another of James's publications – *Counterblaste to Tobacco* – a pamphlet on the evils of smoking, showed him to be very much ahead of his time.) Potts does not appear to have been successful in his attempts to obtain preferment, and nothing further is known of him after 1612.

The work can hardly be described as being impartial. For example, far more space is given to the Pendle Witches, who were convicted and hanged, than to the Samlesbury Witches who were acquitted. Potts uses the latter fact to display the independence and impartiality of the judges. Furthermore, he uses the book to justify the conviction of Jennet Preston at York in July 1612 for having caused the death by witchcraft of Thomas Lister in 1608, having been acquitted at the Lent Assizes in the same year of the murder by witchcraft of murdering a child of one Dodgson. (This had been the subject matter of a separately published pamphlet, but was incorporated into the first edition of Potts' book.)

The story of 'the Lancashire Witches' has been made famous by the books of Harrison Ainsworth (1848) and Robert Neill *Mist over Pendle* 1951). Harrison Ainsworth, as famous as Charles Dickens in his day, was introduced to the story by his friend, James Crossley, who was the Secretary of the Chetham society – Manchester's local history society – and responsible for the reprinting of Potts' book in 1845.

There is one unfortunate misprint in the original book, which refers to the finding of verdicts of 'Not Guilty' in respect of John Bulcock and his mother, Jane Bulcock, but later refers to their execution. The book was printed in some haste, and the Printer draws attention to this at the beginning of the book.

It is somewhat ironic that chronologically the story of the Lancashire Witches really starts in Yorkshire, with the arrest in Gisburn (then in Yorkshire) and the first trial of Jennet Preston at York. Her story is clearly connected with the rest of the Pendle witches, for she is stated as having been at the Good Friday Witches' Sabbat (or coven meeting). She was also the first to be convicted and hanged – before the trial of the others commenced in Lancaster. It is also ironic that the most famous of the witches, Old Demdike (Elizabeth Devise) was never convicted of witchcraft, having escaped the hangman by her death in the dungeons at Lancaster before she could stand trial.

There have been recent calls for the posthumous pardoning of the witches. It must however be remembered that most of them were convicted on their own confessions. Some indeed positively bragged about their powers. However, one of the enigmas in the story is the position of Alice Nutter – a woman of substantial means, unlike the other mostly poverty-stricken characters in the story, and one of those who refused to say anything in her own defence, despite being pressed by the judges to do so. She was convicted of causing the death of Henry Mitton by witchcraft, together with Old Demdike, because he refused to give Demdike the penny that she had begged of him. Why a woman of means would get involved in an offence of this kind is unclear to say the least. Both Harrison Ainsworth and Robert Neill solve the problem by making her the villainess of their respective works. It is now generally thought that the truth is somewhat kinder to Mistress Nutter in that the whole story is bound up with the attempt to establish Protestantism among a superstitious and secretly Catholic people, many of the older ones having been brought up as Catholics. Certainly there were Nutters who had been priests, and had met their deaths for their faith. It is not clear how closely related they were to Alice and her husband, the name being a common one in the area. Certainly many Protestants regarded the Catholic mass and the doctrine of transubstantiation as being examples of witchcraft.

The date of Good Friday may well be significant. Was Alice Nutter on her way to a secret mass rather than a Witches' Sabbat? To have revealed that would not only have put her own life in peril, but those of her Catholic friends as well. Far better to keep silent and face the consequences alone as a secret (and as yet unrecognised) Catholic martyr.

ARTHUR R. D. STUTTARD MA (OXON)
BARRISTER AT LAW
FENCE IN PENDLE

Publishers Note:

This book has been reproduced from a photocopy of the original pamphlet. Due to the variable quality of the photocopied pages, coupled with the age of the original document, the reproduction is not perfect. We apologise for any inconvenience this may cause during the use of this book.

THE
WONDERFVLL
DISCOVERIE OF
WITCHES IN THE COVN-
TIE OF LAN-
CASTER.

With the Arraignement and Triall of
Nineteene notorious WITCHES, at the Assizes and
generall Gaole deliuerie, holden at the Castle of
LANCASTER, *vpon Munday, the se-*
uenteenth of August last,
1 6 1 2.

Before Sir IAMES ALTHAM, and
Sir EDWARD BROMLEY, Knights; BARONS of his
Maiesties Court of EXCHEQVER: And Iustices
of Assize, Oyer and Terminor, *and generall*
Gaole deliuerie in the circuit of the
North Parts.

Together with the Arraignement and Triall of IENNET
PRESTON, *at the Assizes holden at the Castle of Yorke,*
the seuen and twentieth day of Iulie last past,
with her Execution for the murther
of Master LISTER
by Witchcraft.

Published and set forth by commandement of his Maiesties
Iustices of Assize in the North Parts.

By THOMAS POTTS *Esquier.*

LONDON,
Printed by *W. Stansby* for *Iohn Barnes,* dwelling neare
Holborne Conduit. 1613.

TO THE RIGHT HO-

NORABLE, *THOMAS*, LORD
KNYVET, BARON OF ESCRICK
in the Countie of Yorke, my very honorable
good Lord and Master.

AND
TO THE RIGHT HONORABLE
AND VERTVOVS LADIE, THE
Ladie ELIZABETH KNYVET *his Wife, my*
honorable good Ladie and
MISTRIS.

RIGHT HONORABLE,

ET it stand (I beseech
you) with your fauours
whom profession of the
same true Religion to-
wards God, and so great
loue hath vnited together in one, Jointly
to

to accept the Protection and Patronage of these my labours, which not their owne worth hath encouraged, but your Worthinesse hath enforced me to consecrate vnto your Honours.

To you (Right Honourable my very good Lord) of Right doe they belong: for to whom shall I rather present the first fruits of my learning then to your Lordship: who nourished then both mee and them, when there was scarce any being to mee or them? And whose iust and vprght carriage of causes, whose zeale to Iustice and Honourable curtesie to all men, haue purchased you a Reuerend and worthie Respect of all men in all partes of this Kingdome, where you are knowne. And to your good Ladiship
they

Dedicatorie.

they doe of great right belong likewise; Whose Religion, Iustice, and Honourable admittance of my Vnworthie Seruice to your Ladiship doe challenge at my handes the vttermost of what euer I may bee able to performe.

Here is nothing of my own act worthie to bee commended to your Honours, it is the worke, of those Reuerend Magistrates, His Maiesties Iustices of Assizes in the North partes, and no more then a Particular Declaration of the proceedings of Iustice in those partes. Here shall you behold the Iustice of this Land, truely administred, Præmium & Pœnam, Mercie and Iudgement, freely and indifferently bestowed and inflicted; And aboue all things *thinges to bee remembred, the excellent care of these Iudges in the Triall of offendors.*

It hath pleased them out of their respect to mee to impose this worke vpon mee, and according to my vnderstanding, I haue taken paines to finish, and now confirmed by their Iudgement to publish the same, for the benefit of my Countrie. That the example of these conuicted vpon their owne Examinations, Confessions, and Euidence at the Barre, may worke good in others, Rather by with-holding them from, then imboldening them to, the Atcheiuing such desperate actes as these or the like.

These are some part of the fruits of my time spent in the Seruice of my Countrie,

trie, Since by your Graue and Reuerend Counsell (my Good Lord) I reduced my wauering and wandring thoughts to a more quiet harbour of repose.

If it please your Honours to giue them your Honourable respect, the world may iudge them the more worthie of acceptance, to whose various censures they are now exposed.

God of Heauen whose eies are on them that feare him, to bee their Protector and guide, behold your Honours with the eye of fauor, be euermore your strong hold, and your great reward, and blesse you with blessings in this life, Externall and Internall, Temporall and Spirituall, and with Eternall happines in the World to come: to which I commend your Ho-

A *nours;*

nours; And rest both now and euer, From my Lodging in Chancerie Lane, the six-teenth of Nouember 1 6 1 2.

Your Honours

humbly deuoted

Seruant,

Thomas Potts.

Fter he had taken great paines to finish it, J tooke vpon mee to reuise and correct it, that nothing might passe but matter of Fact, apparant againſt them by record. Jt is very little he hath inserted, and that necessarie, to shew what their offences were, what people, and of what condition they were: The whole proceedings and Euidence againſt them, J finde vpon examination carefully set forth, and truely reported, and iudge the worke fit and worthie to be published.

Edward Bromley.

Pon the Arraignement and triall of these Witches at the last Assizes and Generall Gaole-deliuerie, holden at Lancaster, wee found such apparent matters against them, that we thought it necessarie to publish them to the World, and thereupon imposed the labour of this Worke vpon this Gentleman, by reason of his place, being a Clerke at that time in Court, imploied in the Arraignement and triall of them.

Ja. Altham.

Edw. Bromley.

Faults escaped in the Printing.

Page, C 3 : M. *Banester*, for *Bannester*, brough, for brought.
Page, E 2 This people, for these. Page, H Here they parted, for there. page, K 2 these, for this hellish. page, S 3 In the Verdict of Life and Death, Not guiltie, for guiltie. page, S 3 one Horse or Mare, for one Mare in the Indictment. page eadem, for the Triall of her life, reade for the triall of her offence. page, T their view, for your view.

Gentle Reader, although the care of this Gentleman the Author, was great to examine and publish this his worke perfect according to the Honorable testimonie of the Iudges, yet some faults are committed by me in the Printing, and yet not many, being a worke done in such great haste, at the end of a Tearme, which I pray you, with your fauour to excuse.

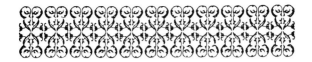

A particular Declaration of

the moſt barberous and damnable Practiſes, Murthers, wicked and diuelish Conspiracies, practized
and executed by the moſt dangerous and malitious
Witch *Elizabeth Sowthernes* alias *Demdike*,
of the Forreſt of *Pendle* in the Countie of
Lancaſter Widdow, who died in the
Caſtle at *Lancaſter* before she
came to receiue her tryall.

Though publique Iuſtice hath passed
at these Assises vpon the Capitall
offendours, and after the Arraignement & tryall of them, Iudgement
being giuen, due and timely Execution succeeded; which doth im-
port and giue the greateſt satisfaction that can be, to all men; yet be-
cause vpon the caryage, and euent of this businesse, the
Eyes of all the partes of *Lancashire*, and other Counties
in the North partes thereunto adioyning were bent: And
so infinite a multitude came to the Arraignement & tryall
of these Witches at *Lancaſter*, the number of them being
knowen to exceed all others at any time heretofore, at one
time to be indicted, arraigned, and receiue their tryall, especially for so many Murders, Conspiracies, Charmes,
Meetinges, hellish and damnable practises, so apparant
vpon their owne examinations & confessions. These my
honourable & worthy Lords, the Iudges of Assise, vpon

B.   great

great consideration, thought it necessarie & profitable, to publish to the whole world, their most barbarous and damnable practises, with the direct proceedinges of the Court against them, as well for that there doe passe diuers vncertaine reportes and relations of such Euidences, as was publiquely giuen against them at their Arraignement. As for that diuers came to prosecute against many of them that were not found guiltie, and so rest very discontented, and not satisfied. As also for that it is necessary for men to know and vnderstande the meanes whereby they worke their mischiefe, the hidden misteries of their diuelish and wicked Inchauntmentes, Charmes, and Sorceries, the better to preuent and auoyde the danger that may ensue. And lastly, who were the principall authors and actors in this late woefull and lamentable *Tragedie*, wherein so much Blood was spilt.

Therefore I pray you giue me leaue, (with your patience and fauour,) before I proceed to the Indictment, Arraignement, and Tryall of such as were Prisoners in the Castle, to lay open the life and death of this damnable and malicious Witch, of so long continuance (old *Demdike*) of whom our whole businesse hath such dependence, that without the particular Declaration and Record of her Euidence, with the circumstaunces, wee shall neuer bring any thing to good perfection : for from this Sincke of villanie and mischiefe, haue all the rest proceeded; as you shall haue them in order.

She was a very old woman, about the age of Fourescore yeares, and had been a Witch for fiftie yeares. Shee dwelt in the Forrest of *Pendle*, a vaste place, fitte for her profession : What shee committed in her time, no man knowes.

Thus liued shee securely for many yeares, brought vp

her

her owne Children, instructed her Graund-children, and tooke great care and paines to bring them to be Witches. Shee was a generall agent for the Deuill in all these partes: no man escaped her, or her Furies, that euer gaue them any occasion of offence, or denyed them any thing they stood need of: And certaine it is, no man neere them, was secure or free from danger.

But God, who had in his diuine prouidence prouided to cut them off, and roote them out of the Common-wealth, so disposed aboue, that the Iustices of those partes, vnderstanding by a generall charme and muttering, the great and vniuersall resort to *Maulking Tower*, the common opinion, with the report of these suspected people, the complaint of the Kinges subiectes for the losse of their Children, Friendes, Goodes, and Cattle, (as there could not be so great Fire without some Smoake,) sent for some of the Countrey, and tooke great paynes to en-quire after their proceedinges, and courses of life.

In the end, *Roger Nowell* Esquire, one of his Maiesties Iustices in these partes, a very religious honest Gentle-man, painefull in the seruice of his Countrey: whose fame for this great seruice to his Countrey, shall liue after him, tooke vpon him to enter into the particular exa-mination of these suspected persons: And to the honour of God, and the great comfort of all his Countrey, made such a discouery of them in order, as the like hath not been heard of: which for your better satisfaction, I haue heere placed in order against her, as they are vpon Record, a-mongst the Recordes of the *Crowne* at *Lancaster*, certified by M. *Nowell*, and others.

The

The voluntarie Confession

and Examination of *Elizabeth Sowtherns* alias
Demdike, taken at the Fence in the Forreſt of *Pendle* in the Countie
of *Lancaſter*.

The second day of Aprill, *Annoq; Regni Regis Iacobi Ang-*
liæ, &c. Decimo, et Scotiæ Quadragesimo quinto ;
Before *Roger Nowell* of *Reade* Esquire, one of his
Maieſties Iuſtices of the peace with-
in the sayd Countie. *Viz.*

THe said *Elizabeth Sowtherns* confesseth, and
sayth; That about twentie yeares paſt, as she
was comming homeward from begging,
there met her this Examinate neere vnto a
Stonepit in *Gouldshey*, in the sayd Forreſt of
Pendle, a Spirit or Deuill in the shape of a Boy, the one
halfe of his Coate blacke, and the other browne, who bade
this Examinate ſtay, saying to her, that if she would giue
him her Soule, she should haue any thing that she would
request. Wherevpon this Examinat demaunded his name?
and the Spirit answered, his name was *Tibb* : and so this
Examinate in hope of such gaine as was promised by the
sayd Deuill or *Tibb*, was contented to giue her Soule to the
said Spirit : And for the space of fiue or sixe yeares next after, the sayd Spirit or Deuill appeared at sundry times vnto
her this Examinate about *Day-light* Gate, alwayes bidding
her ſtay, and asking her this Examinate what she would
haue

haue or doe ? To whom this Examinate replyed, Nay no-
thing : for she this Examinate said, she wanted nothing yet.
And so about the end of the said six yeares, vpon a Sab-
both day in the morning, this Examinate hauing a litle
Child vpon her knee, and she being in a slumber, the sayd
Spirit appeared vnto her in the likenes of a browne Dogg,
forcing himselfe to her knee, to get blood vnder her left
Arme : and she being without any apparrell sauing her
Smocke, the said Deuill did get blood vnder her left arme.
And this Examinate awaking, sayd, *Iesus saue my Child*; but
had no power, nor could not say, *Iesus saue her selfe* : wherevpon the Browne Dogge vanished out of this Examinats
sight : after which, this Examinate was almoſt ſtarke madd
for the space of eight weekes.

And vpon her examination, she further confesseth, and
saith. That a little before Chriſtmas laſt, this Examinates
Daughter hauing been to helpe *Richard Baldwyns* Folkes
at the Mill : This Examinates Daughter did bid her this
Examinate goe to the said *Baldwyns* house, and aske him
some thing for her helping of his Folkes at the Mill, (as
aforesaid :) and in this Examinates going to the said *Baldwyns* house, and neere to the said house, she mette with the
said *Richard Baldwyn* ; Which *Baldwyn* sayd to this Examinate, and the said *Alizon Deuice* (who at that time
ledde this Examinate, being blinde) get out of my ground
Whores and Witches, I will burne the one of you, and
hang the other. To whom this Examinate answered : I
care not for thee, hang thy selfe : Presently wherevpon,
at this Examinates going ouer the next hedge, the said
Spirit or Diuell called *Tibb*, appeared vnto this Examinat,
and sayd, *Reuenge thee of him*. To whom, this Examinate
sayd againe to the said Spirit. *Reuenge thee eyther of him, or
his*. And so the said Spirit vanished out of her sight, and she

neuer saw him since.

And further this Examinate confesseth, and sayth, that the speediest way to take a mans life away by VVitch-craft, is to make a Picture of Clay, like vnto the shape of the person whom they meane to kill, & dry it thorowly : and when they would haue them to be ill in any one place more then an other ; then take a Thorne or Pinne, and pricke it in that part of the Picture you would so haue to be ill : and when you would haue any part of the Body to consume away, then take that part of the Picture, and burne it. And when they would haue the whole body to consume away, then take the remnant of the sayd Picture, and burne it : and so therevpon by that meanes, the body shall die.

The

The Confession and Exami-

nation of Anne Whittle *alias* Chattox, being
Prisoner at *Lancaster*; taken the 19 day of May,
Annoq; Regni Regis Iacobi Anglia, Decimo :
ac Scotie Quadragesimo quinto ; Before
William Sandes Maior of the Bor-
rough towne of *Lancaster.*

Iames Anderton of *Clayton*, one of his Maiesties Iustices
of Peace within the same County, and *Thomas*
Cowell one of his Maiesties Coroners in
the sayd Countie of Lancaster.
Viz.

Irst, the sayd *Anne Whittle*, alias *Chattox*,
sayth, that about fourteene yeares past
she entered, through the wicked perswasions and counsell of *Elizabeth Southerns*,
alias *Demdike*, and was seduced to condis-
cend & agree to become subiect vnto that
diuelish abhominable profession of Witchcraft : Soone
after which, the Deuill appeared vnto her in the liknes of
a Man, about midnight, at the house of the sayd *Demdike* :
and thereupon the sayd *Demdike* and shee, went foorth
of the said house vnto him ; wherevpon the said wicked
Spirit mooued this Examinate, that she would become his
Subiect, and giue her Soule vnto him : the which at first,
she refused to assent vnto ; but after, by the great perswasions made by the sayd *Demdike*, shee yeelded to be at his
commaundement and appoyntment : wherevpon the sayd
wicked Spirit then sayd vnto her, that hee must haue
one part of her body for him to sucke vpon ; the which
shee denyed then to graunt vnto him; and withall asked
him,

him, what part of her body hee would haue for that vse ; who said, hee would haue a place of her right side neere to her ribbes, for him to sucke vpon : whereunto shee assented.

And she further sayth, that at the same time, there was a thing in the likenes of a spotted Bitch, that came with the sayd Spirit vnto the sayd *Demdike*, which then did speake vnto her in this Examinates hearing, and sayd, that she should haue Gould, Siluer, and wordly Wealth, at her will. And at the same time she saith, there was victuals, *viz.* Flesh, Butter, Cheese, Bread, and Drinke, and bidde them eate enough. And after their eating, the Deuill called *Fancie*, and the other Spirit calling himselfe *Tibbe*, carried the remnant away : And she sayeth, that although they did eate, they were neuer the fuller, nor better for the same; and that at their said Banquet, the said Spirits gaue them light to see what they did, although they neyther had fire nor Candle light ; and that they were both shee Spirites, and Diuels.

And being further examined how many sundry Persons haue been bewitched to death, and by whom they were so bewitched : She sayth, that one *Robert Nuter*, late of the *Greene-head* in *Pendle*, was bewitched by this Examinate, the said *Demdike*, and Widdow *Lomshawe*, (late of *Burneley*) now deceased.

And she further sayth, that the said *Demdike* shewed her, that she had bewitched to death, *Richard Ashton*, Sonne of *Richard Ashton* of *Downeham* Esquire.

The

The Examination of Alizon

Deuice, of the Forreƒt of Pendle, in the County
of *Lancaƒter* Spinƒter, taken at *Reade* in the said
Countie of *Lancaƒter, the* xiij. day of
March, *Anno Regni Jacobi Angliæ, &c.*
Nono : et Scotiæ xlv.

Before *Roger Nowell* of *Reade* aforesayd Esquire, one of
his Maieƒties Iuƒtices of the Peace within the sayd
Countie, againƒt *Elizabeth Sowtherns,* alias
Demdike her Grannd-mother.
Viz.

THe sayd *Alizon Deuice* sayth, that about two
yeares agon, her Graund-mother (called
Elizabeth Sowtherns, alias old *Demdike*) did
sundry times in going or walking togeather as they went begging, perswade and
aduise this Examinate to let a Deuill or Familiar appeare
vnto her ; and that shee this Examinate, would let him
sucke at some part of her, and shee might haue, and doe
what shee would.

And she further sayth, that one *Iohn Nutter* of the *Bul-
hole* in *Pendle* aforesaid, had a Cow which was sicke, & re-
queƒted this examinats Grand-mother to amend the said
Cow; and her said Graund-mother said she would, and so
her said Graund-mother about ten of the clocke in the
night, desired this examinate to lead her foorth; which this
Examinate did, being then blind : and her Graund-mother
did remaine about halfe an houre foorth : and this Examinates siƒter did fetch her in againe; but what she did when
she was so foorth, this Examinate cannot tell. But the next

C.   morning,

morning this Examinate heard that the sayd Cow was
dead. And this Examinate verily thinketh, that her sayd
Graund-mother did bewitch the sayd Cow to death.

And further, this Examinate sayth, that about two
yeares agon, this Examinate hauing gotten a Piggin full of
blew Milke by begging, brought it into the house of her
Graund-mother, where (this Examinate going foorth presently, and staying about halfe an houre) there was Butter
to the quantity of a quarterne of a pound in the said milke,
and the quantitie of the said milke still remayning; and her
Graund-mother had no Butter in the house when this Examinate went foorth : duering which time, this Examinates Graund-mother still lay in her bed.

And further this Examinate sayth, that *Richard Baldwin*
of *Weethead* within the Forrest of *Pendle*, about 2. yeeres
agoe, fell out with this Examinates Graund-mother, & so
would not let her come vpon his Land : and about foure
or fiue dayes then next after, her said Graund-mother did
request this Examinate to lead her foorth about ten of the
clocke in the night : which this Examinate accordingly
did, and she stayed foorth then about an houre, and this
Examinates sister fetched her in againe. And this Examinate heard the next morning, that a woman Child of the
sayd *Richard Baldwins* was fallen sicke ; and as this Examinate did then heare, the sayd Child did languish afterwards by the space of a yeare, or thereaboutes, and dyed:
And this Examinate verily thinketh, that her said Graund-
mother did bewitch the sayd Child to death.

And further, this Examinate sayth, that she heard her
sayd Graund-mother say presently after her falling out
with the sayd *Baldwin*, shee would pray for the sayd *Baldwin* both still and loude : and this Examinate heard her
cursse the sayd *Baldwin* sundry times.

                                                        The

THE sayd Examinate *Iames Deuice* sayth, that about a month agoe, as this Examinate was comming towards his Mothers house, and at day-gate of the same night, this Examinate mette a browne Dogge comming from his Graund-mothers house, about tenne Roodes diſtant from the same house : and about two or three nights after, that this Examinate heard a voyce of a great number of Children screiking and crying pittifully, about day-light gate ; and likewise, about ten Roodes diſtant of this Examinates sayd Graund-mothers house. And about fiue nights then next following, presently after daylight, within 20. Roodes of the sayd *Elizabeth Sowtherns* house, he heard a foule yelling like vnto a great number of Cattes : but what they were, this Examinate cannot tell. And he further sayth, that about three nights after that, about midnight of the same, there came a thing, and lay vpon him very heauily about an houre, and went then from him out of his Chamber window, coloured blacke, and about the bignesse of a Hare or Catte. And he further sayth, that about S. *Peters* day laſt, one *Henry Bullocke* came to the sayd *Elizabeth Sowtherns* house, and sayd, that her Graund-child *Alizon Deuice,* had bewitched a Child of his, and desired her that she would goe with him to his house ; which accordingly she did : And there-vpon she the said *Alizon* fell downe on her knees, & asked the said *Bullocke* forgiuenes, and confessed to him, that she had bewitched the said child, as this Examinate heard his said siſter confesse vnto him this Examinate.

The

The Examination of Eliza-

beth Deuice, Daughtor of old Demdike, taken
at *Read* before *Roger Nowell* Esquire, one of
his Maiesties Iustices of Peace within the
Countie of *Lancaster* the xxx. day
of March, *Annoq̃ Regni Jacobi*
Decimo, ac Scotie xlv.

He sayd *Elizabeth Deuice* the Exa-
minate, sayth, that the sayd *Eliza-*
beth Sowtherns, alias *Demdike*, hath
had a place on her left side by the
space of fourty yeares, in such sort,
as was to be seene at this Examinates Examination taking, at this
present time.

Heere this worthy Iustice M. *Nowell*, out of these particular Examinations, or rather Accusations, finding matter to proceed; and hauing now before him old *Demdike*,
old *Chattox*, *Alizon Deuice*, and *Redferne* both old and
young, *Reos confitentes, et Accusantes Inuicem*. About the
second of Aprill last past, committed and sent them away
to the Castle at *Lancaster*, there to remaine vntill the comming of the Kinges Maiesties Iustices of Assise, then to
receiue their tryall.

But

But heere they had not ſtayed a weeke, when their
Children and Friendes being abroad at libertie, laboured a
speciall meeting at *Malking Tower* in the Forreſt of *Pendle*, vpon Good-fryday, within a weeke after they were
committed, of all the moſt dangerous, wicked, and damnable Witches in the County farre and neere. Vpon
Good-fryday they met, according to solemne appoyntment, solemnized this great Feaſtiuall day according to
their former order, with great cheare, merry company,
and much conference.

In the end, in this great Assemblie, it was decreed M.
Couell by reason of his Office, shall be slaine before the
next Assises: The Caſtle of *Lancaſter* to be blowen vp,
and ayde and assiſtance to be sent to kill M. *Liſter*, with
his old Enemie and wicked Neighbour *Iennet Preſton*;
with some other such like praĉtises: as vpon their Arraignement and Tryall, are particularly set foorth, and giuen in euidence againſt them.

This was not so secret, but some notice of it came to M.
Nowell, and by his great paines taken in the Examination
of *Iennet Deuice*, al their praĉtises are now made knowen.
Their purpose to kill M. *Couell*, and blow vp the Caſtle,
is preuented. All their Murders, Witchcraftes, Inchauntments, Charmes, & Sorceries, are discouered; and euen in
the middeſt of their Consultations, they are all confoun-
ded, and arreſted by Gods Iuſtice: brough before M.
Nowell, and M. *Baueſter*, vpon their voluntary confessions, Examinations, and other Euidence accused, and so
by them committed to the Caſtle: So as now both old
and young, haue taken vp their lodgings with M. *Couell*,
vntill the next Assises, expeĉting their Tryall and deli-
ueraunce, according to the Lawes prouided for such
like.

In the meane time, M. *Nowell* hauing knowledge by this discouery of their meeting at *Malking Tower*, and their resolution to execute mischiefe, takes great paines to apprehend such as were at libertie, and prepared Euidence against all such as were in question for Witches.

Afterwardes sendes some of these Examinations, to the Assises at Yorke, to be giuen in Euidence against *Iennet Preston*, who for the murder of M. *Lister*, is condemned and executed.

The Circuite of the North partes being now almost ended.

The 16. of August.

Vpon Sunday in the after noone, my honorable Lords the Iudges of Assise, came from *Kendall* to *Lancaster*.

Wherevpon M. *Couell* presented vnto their Lordships a Calender, conteyning the Names of the Prisoners committed to his charge, which were to receiue their Tryall at the Assises : Out of which, we are onely to deale with the proceedings against Witches, which were as followeth. *Viz.*

The

The Names of the

Witches committed to the Castle of *Lancaster.*

Elizabeth Southerns. alias *Old Demdike.*	Who dyed before shee came to her tryall.

Anne Whittle, alias *Chattox*,

Elizabeth Deuice, Daughter of old *Demdike.*

Iames Deuice, Sonne of *Elizabeth Deuice.*

Anne Readfearne, Daughter of *Anne Chattox.*

Alice Nutter.

Katherine Hewytte.

Iohn Bulcocke.

Iane Bulcocke.

Alizon Deuice, Daughter of *Elizabeth Deuice.*

Isabell Robey.

Margaret Pearson.

The Witches of Salmesbury.

Iennet Bierley. *Elen Bierley.* *Iane Southworth.* *Iohn Ramesden.*	*Elizabeth Astley.* *Alice Gray.* *Isabell Sidegraues.* *Lawrence Haye.*

The next day, being Monday, the 17. of August, were the Assises holden in the Castle of *Lancaster* as followeth.

Placita

PLACITA CORONÆ,
Apud Lancaſterium.

DEliberatio *Gaolæ Domini Regis Caſtri sui Lancaſtrii ac Prisonarioru͂ in eadem exiſtent. Tenta apud Lanca-ſterium in com. Lancaſterij. Die Lunæ, Decimo septimo die Auguſti, Anno Regni Domini noſtri Iacobi dei gratiæ Angliæ, Franciæ, et Hiberniæ, Regis fidei defensoris; Decimo: et Scotiæ Quadragesimo sexto; Coram Iacobo Al-tham Milit. vno Baronum Scaccarij Domini Regis, et Ed-wardo Bromley Milit. altero Barono, eiusdem Scaccarij Domini Regis: ac Iuſtic. Domini Regis apud Lancaſtr.*

VPon the Tewesday in the after noone, the Iudges according to the course and order, deuided themselues, where-vpon my Lord *Bromley*, one of his Maieſtices Iudges of Assise comming into the Hall to proceede with the Pleaes of the Crowne, & the Arraigne-ment and Tryall of Prisoners, commaunded a generall Proclamation, that all Iuſtices of Peace that had taken any Recognisaunces, or Examinations of Prisoners, should make Returne of them: And all such as were bound to prosecute Indictmentes, and giue Euidence againſt Witches, should proceede, and giue attendance: For hee now intended to proceed to the Arraignement and Tryall of VVitches.

After which, the Court being set, M. Sherieffe was commaunded to present his Prisoners before his Lord-ship, and prepare a sufficient Iurie of Gentlemen for life and death. But heere we want old *Demdike*, who dyed in the Caſtle before she came to her Tryall.

Heere

Heere you may not expeƈt the exaƈt order of the Assises, with the Proclamations, and other solemnities belonging to so great a Court of Iuſtice ; but the proceedinges againſt the Witches, who are now vpon their deliuerance here in order as they came to the Barre, with the particular poyntes of Euidence againſt them: which is the labour and worke we now intend (by Gods grace) to performe as we may, to your generall contentment.

Wherevpon, the firſt of all these, *Anne Whittle*, alias *Chattox*, was brought to the Barre : againſt whom wee are now ready to proceed.

The

D.

The Arraignement and

Tryall of Anne Whittle, *alias* Chattox,
of the Forreſt of *Pendle*, in the Countie of *Lancaſter*, Widdow ;
about the age of Foure-
score yeares, or there-
aboutes.

Anne Whittle, alias *Chattox*.

IF in this damnable course of life, and offences, more horrible and odious, then any
man is able to expresse : any man lyuing
could lament the estate of any such like
vpon earth : The example of this poore
creature, would haue moued pittie, in re-
speƈt of her great contrition and repentance, after she was
committed to the Caſtle at *Lancaſter*, vntill the comming
of his Maieſties Iudges of Assise. But such was the nature of her offences, & the multitude of her crying sinnes,
as it tooke away all sense of humanity. And the repeti-
tion of her hellish praƈtises, and Reuenge; being the chie-
feſt thinges wherein she alwayes tooke great delight, togeather with a particular declaration of the Murders shee
had committed, layde open to the world, and giuen in
Euidence againſt her at the time of her Arraignement and
Tryall ;

Tryall ; as certainely it did beget contempt in the Audience, and such as she neuer offended.

This *Anne Whittle*, alias *Chattox*, was a very old withered spent & decreped creature, her sight almost gone: A dangerous Witch, of very long continuance ; alwayes opposite to old *Demdike* : For whom the one fauoured, *Her o*
the other hated deadly : and how they enuie and accuse *exami*
one an other, in their Examinations, may appeare.

In her Witchcraft, alwayes more ready to doe mischiefe to mens goods, then themselues. Her lippes euer chattering and walking : but no man knew what. She liued in the Forreſt of *Pendle*, amongſt this wicked company of dangerous Witches. Yet in her Examination and Confession, she dealt alwayes very plainely and truely : for vpon a speciall occasion being oftentimes examined in open Court, shee was neuer found to vary, but alwayes to agree in one, and the selfe same thing.

I place her in order, next to that wicked fire-brand of mischiefe, old *Demdike*, because from these two, sprung all the rest in order : and were the Children and Friendes, of these two notorious VVitches.

Many thinges in the discouery of them, shall be very worthy your obseruation. As the times and occasions to execute their mischiefe. And this in generall : the Spirit could neuer hurt, till they gaue consent.

And, but that it is my charge, to set foorth a particular Declaration of the Euidence againſt them, vpon their Arraignement and Tryall; with their Diuelish praƈtises, consultations, meetings, and murders committed by them,

in

in such sort, as they were giuen in Euidence against them; for the which, I shall haue matter vpon Record. I could make a large Comentarie of them : But it is my humble duety, to obserue the Charge and Commaundement of these my Honorable good Lordes the Iudges of Assise, and not to exceed the limits of my Commission. Wherefore I shall now bring this auncient Witch, to the due course of her Tryall, in order.   *viz.*

Indictment.

THis *Anne Whittle*, alias *Chattox*, of the Forrest of *Pendle* in the Countie of *Lancaster* Widdow, being Indicted, for that shee feloniously had practised, vsed, and exercised diuers wicked and diuelish Artes called Witchcraftes, Inchauntmentes, Charmes, and Sorceries, in and vpon one *Robert Nutter* of *Greenehead*, in the Forrest of *Pendle*, in the Countie of *Lanc* : and by force of the same Witchcraft, feloniously the sayd *Robert Nutter* had killed, *Contra Pacem, &c.* Being at the Barre, was arraigned.

To this Indictment, vpon her Arraignement, shee pleaded, Not guiltie : and for the tryall of her life, put her selfe vpon God and her Country.

Wherevpon my Lord *Bromley* commaunded M. Sheriffe of the County of *Lancaster* in open Court, to returne a Iurie of worthy sufficient Gentlemen of vnderstanding, to passe betweene our soueraigne Lord the Kinges Maiestie, and her, and others the Prisoners, vpon their liues and deathes ; as hereafter follow in order : who were afterwardes sworne, according to the forme and order of the

the Court, the Prisoners being admitted to their lawfull challenges.

VVhich being done, and the Prisoner at the Barre readie to receiue her Tryall : M. *Nowell*, being the best instructed of any man, of all the particular poyntes of Euidence against her, and her fellowes, hauing taken great paynes in the proceedinges against her and her fellowes; Humbly prayed, her owne voluntary Confession and Examination taken before him, when she was apprehended and committed to the Castle of *Lancaster* for Witchcraft; might openly be published against her: which hereafter followeth. *Viz.*

The voluntary Confession and examination of *Anne Whittle*, alias *Chattox*, taken at the *Fence* in the Forrest of *Pendle*, in the Countie of *Lancaster*; Before *Roger Nowell Esq*, one of the Kinges Maiesties Iustices of Peace in the Countie of Lancaster. Viz.

THe sayd *Anne Whittle*, alias *Chattox*, vpon her Examination, voluntarily confesseth, and sayth, That about foureteene or fifteene yeares agoe, a thing like a Christian man for foure yeares togeather, did sundry times come to this Examinate, and requested this Examinate to giue him her Soule: And in the end, this Examinate was contented to giue him her sayd Soule, shee being then in her owne house, in the Forrest of *Pendle* ; wherevpon the Deuill then in the shape of a Man, sayd to this Examinate: Thou shalt want nothing ; and be reuenged of whom thou list. And the Deuill then further com-

maun-

maunded this Examinate, to call him by the name of *Fancie* ; and when she wanted any thing, or would be reuenged of any, call on *Fancie*, and he would be ready. And the sayd Spirit or Deuill, ˙ ˙d appeare vnto her not long after, in mans likenesse, and would haue had this Examinate to haue consented, that he might hurt the wife of *Richard Baldwin* of *Pendle* ; But this Examinate would not then consent vnto him : For which cause, the sayd Deuill would then haue bitten her by the arme ; and so vanished away, for that time.

And this Examinate further sayth, that *Robert Nutter* did desire her Daughter one *Redfearns* wife, to haue his pleasure of her, being then in *Redfearns* house : but the sayd *Redfearns* wife denyed the sayd *Robert ;* wherevpon the sayd *Robert* seeming to be greatly displeased therewith, in a great anger tooke his Horse, and went away, saying in a great rage, that if euer the Ground came to him, shee should neuer dwell vpon his Land. Wherevpon this Examinate called *Fancie* to her ; who came to her in the likenesse of a Man in a parcell of Ground called, *The Laund* ; asking this Examinate, what shee would haue him to doe ? And this Examinate bade him goe reuenge her of the sayd *Robert Nutter*. After which time, the sayd *Robert Nutter* liued about a quarter of a yeare, and then dyed.

And this Examinate further sayth, that *Elizabeth Nutter*, wife to old *Robert Nutter*, did request this Examinate, and *Loomeshaws* wife of *Burley*, and one *Iane Boothman*, of the same, who are now both dead, (which time of request, was before that *Robert Nutter* desired the company of *Redfearns* wife) to get young *Robert Nutter* his death, if
                                                                they

they could; all being togeather then at that time, to that
end, that if *Robert* were dead, then the Women their
Coosens might haue the Land: By whose perswasion, they
all consented vnto it. After which time, this Examinates
Sonne in law *Thomas Redfearne*, did perswade this Examinate, not to kill or hurt the sayd *Robert Nutter* ; for
which perswasion, the sayd *Loomeshaws* Wife, had like to
haue killed the sayd *Redfearne*, but that one M. *Baldwyn*
(the late Schoole-maiſter at *Coulne*) did by his learning,
ſtay the sayd *Loomeshaws* wife, and therefore had a Capon
from *Redfearne*.

And this Examinate further sayth, that she thinketh the
sayd *Loomeshaws* wife, and *Iane Boothman*, did what they
could to kill the sayd *Robert Nutter*, as well as this Examinate did.

The

The Examination of ELIZABETH SOTHERNES, alias OLD DEMBDIKE: *taken at the Fence in the Forrest of Pendle in the Countie of Lancaster, the day and yeare aforesaid.*

Before,

ROGER NOWEL *Esquire, one of the Kings Maiesties Iustices of Peace in the said Countie, against* ANNE WHITTLE, alias CHATTOX.

THe said *Elizabeth Southernes* saith vpon her Examination, that about halfe a yeare before *Robert Nutter* died, as this Examinate thinketh, this Examinate went to the house of *Thomas Redfearne*, which was about Mid-sommer, as this Examinate remembreth it. And there within three yards of the East end of the said house, shee saw the said *Anne Whittle*, alias *Chattox*, and *Anne Redferne* wife of the said *Thomas Redferne*, and Daughter of the said *Anne Whittle*, alias *Chattox:* the one on the one side of the Ditch, and the other on the other : and two Pictures of Clay or Marle lying by them : and the third Picture the said *Anne Whittle*, alias *Chattox*, was making : and the said *Anne Redferne* her said Daughter, wrought her Clay or Marle to make the third picture withall. And this Examinate passing by them, the said Spirit, called *Tibb*, in the shape of a black Cat, appeared vnto her this Examinate, and said, turne back againe, and doe as they doe : To whom this Examinate said, what are they doing ? whereunto the said Spirit said ; they are making three Pictures : whereupon she asked whose pictures they were ? whereunto the said Spirit said : they

E   are

are the pictures of *Chriſtopher Nutter*, *Robert Nutter*, and
Marie, wife of the said *Robert Nutter* : But this Examinate denying to goe back to helpe them to make the Pictures aforesaid ; the said Spirit seeming to be angrie,
therefore shoue or pushed this Examinate into the
ditch, and so shed the Milke which this Examinate had
in a Can or Kit : and so thereupon the Spirit at that time
vanished out of this Examinates sight : But presently after that, the said Spirit appeared to this Examinate a-
gaine in the shape of a Hare, and so went with her a-
bout a quarter of a mile, but said nothing to this Examinate, nor shee to it.

The Examination and euidence of IAMES
ROBINSON, *taken the day and yeare aforesaid.*

Before
ROGER NOWEL *Esquire aforesaid, againſt* ANNE
WHITTLE, alias CHATTOX, *Prisoner at the Barre
as followeth.* viz.

THe said Examinate saith, that about six yeares a-
goe, *Anne Whittle*, alias *Chattox*, was hired by this
Examinates wife to card wooll ; and so vpon a Friday
and Saturday, shee came and carded wooll with this Examinates wife, and so the Munday then next after shee
came likewise to card : and this Examinates wife hauing
newly tunned drinke into Stands, which ſtood by the
said *Anne Whittle*, alias *Chattox :* and the said *Anne Whittle*
taking a Dish or Cup, and drawing drinke seuerall times:
                                                    and

and so neuer after that time, for some eight or nine
weekes, they could haue any drinke, but spoiled, and as
this Examinate thinketh was by the meanes of the said
Chattox. And further he saith, that the said *Anne Whittle*,
alias *Chattox*, and *Anne Redferne* her said Daughter,
are commonly reputed and reported to bee Witches.
And hee also saith, that about some eighteene yeares a-
goe, he dwelled with one *Robert Nutter* the elder, of
Pendle aforesaid. And that yong *Robert Nutter*, who
dwelled with his Grand-father, in the Sommer time, he
fell sicke, and in his said sicknesse hee did seuerall times
complaine, that hee had harme by them : and this Examinate asking him what hee meant by that word *Them*,
He said, that he verily thought that the said *Anne Whittle*, alias *Chattox*, and the said *Redfernes* wife, had bewitched him : and the said *Robert Nutter* shortly after,
being to goe with his then Maſter, called Sir *Richard
Shattleworth*, into Wales, this Examinate heard him
say before his then going, vnto the said *Thomas Redferne*, that if euer he came againe he would get his Father to put the said *Redferne* out of his house, or he himselfe would pull it downe ; to whom the said *Redferne*
replyed, saying ; when you come back againe you will
be in a better minde : but he neuer came back againe, but
died before Candlemas in Cheshire, as he was comming
homeward.

Since the voluntarie confession and examination of a
Witch, doth exceede all other euidence, I spare to
trouble you with a multitude of Examinations,
or Depositions of any other witnesses, by reason of
this bloudie faɕt, for the Murder of *Robert Nutter*,
vpon so small an occasion, as to threaten to take away

his

his owne land from such as were not worthie to inha-
bite or dwell vpon it, is now made by that which you
haue alreadie heard, so apparant, as no indifferent man
will question it, or rest vnsatisfied : I shall now proceede
to set forth vnto you the rest of her actions, remaining
vpon Record. And how dangerous it was for any man
to liue neere this people, to giue them any occasion of
offence, I leaue it to your good consideration.

The Examination and voluntarie Con-

fession of ANNE WHITTLE, *alias* CHATTOX, *ta-*
ken at the Fence in the Forrest of Pendle, in the Countie
of Lancaster, the second day of April, Anno Regni
Regis IACOBI Angliæ, Franciæ, & Hiberniæ, decimo, & Scotiæ xlv.

Before

ROGER NOVVEL, *Esquire, one of his Maiesties*
Iustices of Peace within the Countie of Lancaster.

SHe the said Examinate saith, That shee was sent for
by the wife of *Iohn Moore*, to helpe drinke that was
forspoken or bewitched : at which time shee vsed this
Prayer for the amending of it, *viz.*

A Charme.

Three Biters hast thou bitten,
  The Hart, ill Eye, ill Tonge :

Three

Three bitter fhall be thy Boote,
    Father, Sonne, and Holy Ghoft
       a Gods name.
    Fiue Pater-nofters, fiue Auies,
       and a Creede,
    In worfhip of fiue wounds
       of our Lord.

After which time that this Examinate had vsed these prayers, and amended her drinke, the said *Moores* wife did chide this Examinate, and was grieued at her.

And thereupon this Examinate called for her Deuill *Fancie*, and bad him goe bite a browne Cow of the said *Moores* by the head, and make the Cow goe madde : and the Deuill then, in the likenesse of a browne Dogge, went to the said Cow, and bit her : which Cow went madde accordingly, and died within six weekes next after, or thereabouts.

Also this Examinate saith, That shee perceiuing *Anthonie Nutter* of Pendle to fauour *Elizabeth Sothernes*, alias *Dembdike*, she, this Examinate, called *Fancie* to her, (who appeared like a man) and bad him goe kill a Cow of the said *Anthonies* ; which the said Deuill did, and that Cow died also.

And further this Examinate saith, That the Deuill, or *Fancie*, hath taken moft of her sight away from her. And further this Examinate saith, That in Summer last, saue one, the said Deuill, or *Fancie*, came vpon this Examinate in the night time : and at diuerse and sundry times in the likenesse of a Beare, gaping as though he would haue wearied this Examinate. And the laft time of all shee, this Examinate, saw him, was vpon

E 3   Thurs-

Thursday laſt yeare but one, next before Midsummer day, in the euening, like a Beare, and this Examinate would not then speake vnto him, for the which the said Deuill pulled this Examinate downe.

The Examination of IAMES DEVICE,

sonne of ELIZABETH DEVICE, *taken the seuen and twentieth day of Aprill*, Annoq; Reg. Regis IACOBI Angliæ, &c. Decimo ac Scotiæ xlv.

Before

ROGER NOVVEL and NICHOLAS BANISTER, *Esquires, two of his* Maieſlies *Iuſlices of the Peace within the said Countie.* viz.

ANd further saith, That twelue yeares agoe, the said *Anne Chattox* at a Buriall at the new Church in Pendle, did take three scalpes of people, which had been buried, and then caſt out of a graue, as she the said *Chattox* told this Examinate; and tooke eight teeth out of the said Scalpes, whereof she kept foure to her selfe, and gaue other foure to the said *Demdike*, this Examinates Grand-mother : which foure teeth now shewed to this Examinate, are the foure teeth that the said *Chattox* gaue to his said Grand-mother, as aforesaid ; which said teeth haue euer since beene kept, vntill now found by the said *Henry Hargreiues* & this Examinate, at the Weſt-end of this Examinates Grand-mothers house, and there buried in the earth, and a Picture of Clay there likewise found by them, about halfe a yard ouer in the earth.

earth, where the said teeth lay, which said picture so found, was almost withered away, and was the Picture of *Anne*, *Anthony Nutters* daughter; as this Examinates Grand-mother told him.

The Examination of ALLIZON DE-VICE *daughter of* ELIZABETH DEVICE: *Taken at Reade, in the Countie of Lancaster, the thirtieth day of March,* Annoq; Reg. Regis IACOBI nunc Angliæ, &c. Decimo, & Scotiæ Quadragesimo quinto.

Before

ROGER NOVVEL *of Reade aforesaid, Esquire, one of his Maiesties Iustices of the Peace, within the said Countie.*

THis Examinate saith, That about eleuen yeares a-goe, this Examinate and her mother had their fire-house broken, and all, or the most part of their linnen clothes, & halfe a peck of cut oat-meale, and a quantitie of meale gone, all which was worth twentie shillings or aboue: and vpon a Sunday then next after, this Examinate did take a band and a coife, parcell of the goods a-foresaid, vpon the daughter of *Anne Whittle*, *alias Chat-tox*, and claimed them to be parcell of the goods stolne, as aforesaid.

And this Examinate further saith, That her father, called *Iohn Deuice*, being afraid, that the said *Anne Chat-tox* should doe him or his goods any hurt by Witchcraft;

craft; did couenant with the said *Anne*, that if she would hurt neither of them, she should yearely haue one Agh-en-dole of meale; which meale was yearely paid, vntill the yeare which her father died in, which was about e-leuen yeares since: Her father vpon his then-death-bed, taking it that the said *Anne Whittle*, alias *Chattox*, did be-witch him to death, because the said meale was not paid the last yeare.

And she also saith, That about two yeares agone, this Examinate being in the house of *Anthony Nutter* of Pendle aforesaid, and being then in company with *Anne Nutter*, daughter of the said *Anthony*: the said *Anne Whittle*, alias *Chattox*, came into the said *Anthony Nutters* house, and seeing this Examinate, and the said *Anne Nutter* laughing, and saying, that they laughed at her the said *Chattox*: well said then (sayes *Anne Chattox*) I will be meet with the one of you. And vpon the next day after, she the said *Anne Nutter* fell sicke, and within three weekes after died. And further, this Examinate saith, That about two yeares agoe, she, this Examinate, hath heard, That the said *Anne Whittle*, alias *Chattox*, was suspected for bewitching the drinke of *Iohn Moore* of Higham Gentleman: and not long after, shee this Exa-minate heard the said *Chattox* say, that she would meet with the said *Iohn Moore*, or his. Whereupon a child of the said *Iohn Moores*, called *Iohn*, fell sicke, and anguished about halfe a yeare, and then died: during which lan-guishing, this Examinate saw the said *Chattox* sitting in her owne garden, and a picture of Clay like vnto a child in her Apron; which this Examinate espying, the said *Anne Chattox* would haue hidde with her Apron: and this Examinate declaring the same to her mother, her

mother

mother thought it was the picture of the said *Iohn Moores* childe.

And she this Examinate further saith, That about sixe or seuen yeares agoe, the said *Chattox* did fall out with one *Hugh Moore* of Pendle, as aforesaid, about certaine cattell of the said *Moores*, which the said *Moore* did charge the said *Chattox* to haue bewitched: for which the said *Chattox* did curse and worry the said *Moore*, and said she would be Reuenged of the said *Moore*: whereupon the said *Moore* presently fell sicke, and languished about halfe a yeare, and then died. Which *Moore* vpon his death-bed said, that the said *Chattox* had bewitched him to death. And she further saith, That about sixe yeares agoe, a daughter of the said *Anne Chattox*, called *Elizabeth*, hauing been at the house of *Iohn Nutter* of the Bull-hole, to begge or get a dish full of milke, which she had, and brought to her mother, who was about a fields breadth of the said *Nutters* house, which her said mother *Anne Chattox* tooke and put into a Kan, and did charne the same with two stickes acrosse in the same field: whereupon the said *Iohn Nutters* sonne came vnto her, the said *Chattox*, and misliking her doings, put the said Kan and milke ouer with his foot; and the morning next after, a Cow of the said *Iohn Nutters* fell sicke, and so languished three or foure dayes, and then died.

In the end being openly charged with all this in open Court; with weeping teares she humbly acknowledged them to be true, and cried out vnto God for Mercy and forgiuenesse of her sinnes, and humbly prayed my Lord to be mercifull vnto *Anne Redfearne* her daughter, of whose life and condition you shall heare more vpon

F   her

her Arraignement and Triall : whereupon shee being
taken away, *Elizabeth Deuice* comes now to receiue
her Triall being the next in order, of whom
you shall heare at
large.

———————————————

———————————————

THE

THE ARRAIGNMENT

and Triall of ELIZABETH DE-
VICE *(Daughter of* ELIZABETH SOTHERNES,
alias OLD DEMBDIKE) *late wife of* IO. DEVICE,
*of the Forrest of Pendle, in the Countie of Lancaster, wi-
dow, for Witchcraft ; Vpon Tuesday the eighteenth of August, at the Assises and generall Gaole-Deliuerie holden at
Lancaster*

Before

Sir EDVVARD BROMLEY *Knight, one of his Maiesties Iustices of Assise at Lancaster.*

Elizabeth Deuice.

OBarbarous and inhumane Monster, beyond example ; so farre from sensible vnderstanding of thy owne miserie, as to
bring thy owne naturall children into
mischiefe and bondage ; and thy selfe to
be a witnesse vpon the Gallowes, to see thy owne children, by thy deuillish instructions hatcht vp in Villanie
and Witchcraft, to suffer with thee, euen in the beginning of their time, a shamefull and vntimely Death.
Too much (so it be true) cannot be said or written of
her. Such was her life and condition : that euen at the
Barre, when shee came to receiue her Triall (where the

least

least sparke of Grace or modestie would haue procured fauour, or moued pitie) she was not able to containe her selfe within the limits of any order or gouernment : but exclaiming, in very outragious manner crying out a-gainst her owne children, and such as came to prosecute Indictments & Euidence for the Kings Maiestie against her, for the death of their Children, Friends, and Kins-folkes, whome cruelly and bloudily, by her Enchaunt-ments, Charmes, and Sorceries she had murthered and cut off ; sparing no man with fearefull execrable curses and banning : Such in generall was the common opini-on of the Countrey where she dwelt, in the Forrest of Pendle (a place fit for people of such condition) that no man neere her, neither his wife, children, goods, or cat-tell should be secure or free from danger.

This *Elizabeth Deuice* was the daughter of *Elizabeth Sothernes*, old *Dembdike*, a malicious, wicked, and dange-rous Witch for fiftie yeares, as appeareth by Record : and how much longer, the Deuill and shee knew best, with whome shee made her couenant.

It is very certaine, that amongst all these Witches there was not a more dangerous and deuillish Witch to execute mischiefe, hauing old *Dembdike*, her mother, to assist her ; *Iames Deuice* and *Alizon Deuice*, her owne na-turall children, all prouided with Spirits, vpon any occa-sion of offence readie to assist her.

Vpon her Examination, although Master *Nowel* was very circumspect, and exceeding carefull in dealing with her, yet she would confesse nothing, vntill it plea-sed God to raise vp a yong maid, *Iennet Deuice*, her owne daughter, about the age of nine yeares (a witnesse vn-expected) to discouer all their Practises, Meetings, Consultations,

sultations, Murthers, Charmes, and Villanies : such, and in such sort, as I may iustly say of them, as a reuerend and learned Iudge of this Kingdome speaketh of the greatest Treason that euer was in this Kingdome, *Quis hæc posterìs sic narrare poterit, vt facta non ficta esse videantur ?* That when these things shall be related to Posteritie, they will be reputed matters fained, not done.

And then knowing, that both *Iennet Deuice,* her daughter, *Iames Deuice,* her sonne, and *Alizon Deuice,* with others, had accused her and layd open all things, in their Examinations taken before Master *Nowel,* and although she were their owne naturall mother, yet they did not spare to accuse her of euery particular fact, which in her time she had committed, to their knowledge ; she made a very liberall and voluntarie Confession, as hereafter shall be giuen in euidence against her, vpon her Arraignment and Triall.

This *Elizabeth Deuice* being at libertie, after Old *Dembdike* her mother, *Alizon Deuice,* her daughter, and old *Chattocks* were committed to the Castle of Lancaster for Witchcraft ; laboured not a little to procure a solemne meeting at Malkyn-Tower of the Graund Witches of the Counties of Lancaster and Yorke, being yet vnsuspected and vntaken, to consult of some speedie course for the deliuerance of their friends, the Witches at Lancaster, and for the putting in execution of some other deuillish practises of Murther and Mischiefe : as vpon the Arraignement and Triall of *Iames Deuice,* her sonne, shall hereafter in euery particular point appeare at large against her.

The

The first Indictment.

THis *Elizabeth Deuice*, late the wife of *Iohn Deuice*, of the Forrest of Pendle, in the Countie of Lancaster Widdow, being indicted, for that shee felloniously had practized, vsed, and exercised diuers wicked and deuillish Arts, called *Witch-crafts*, *Inchantments*, *Charmes*, and *Sorceries*, in, and vpon one *Iohn Robinson*, alias *Swyer :* and by force of the same felloniously, the said *Iohn Rabinson*, alias *Swyer*, had killed. *Contra pacem, &c.* being at the Barre was arraigned.

2. Indictment.

The said *Elizabeth Deuice* was the second time indicted in the same manner and forme, for the death of *Iames Robinson*, by Witch-craft. *Contra pacem, &c.*

3. Indictment.

The said *Elizabeth Deuice*, was the third time with others, *viz. Alice Nutter*, and *Elizabeth Sothernes*, alias *Old-Dembdike*, her Grand-mother, Indicted in the same manner and forme, for the death of *Henrie Mytton*. *Contra pacem, &c.*

To these three seuerall Indictments vpon her Arraignment, shee pleaded not guiltie ; and for the tryall of her life, put her selfe vpon God and her Countrie.

So as now the Gentlemen of the Iurie of life and death, stand charged to finde, whether shee bee guiltie of them, or any of them.

Where-

Whereupon there was openly read, and giuen in e-
uidence against her, for the Kings Maiestie, her owne
voluntarie Confession and Examination, when shee was
apprehended, taken, and committed to the Castle of
Lancaster by M. *Nowel*, and M. *Bannester*, two of his
Maiesties Iustices of Peace in the same Countie. *viz.*

The Examination and voluntarie confes-
sion of ELIZABETH DEVICE, *taken at the house of*
IAMES WILSEY *of the Forrest of Pendle, in the Coun-*
tie of Lancaster, the seuen and twentieth day of Aprill :
Anno Reg. IACOBI, *Angl. &c. decimo, & Scotiæ* xlv.

Before

ROGER NOWEL, *and* NICHOLAS BANNE-
STER, *Esquires* ; *two of his Maiesties Iustices of the Peace*
within the same Countie. viz.

The said *Elizabeth Deuice*, Mother of the said
Iames, being examined, confesseth and saith.

THat at the third time her Spirit, the Spirit *Ball*, appeared to her in the shape of a browne Dogge, at, or
in her Mothers house in Pendle Forrest aforesaid : about
foure yeares agoe the said Spirit bidde this Examinate
make a picture of Clay, after the said *Iohn Robinson*, alias
Swyer, which this Examinate did make accordingly at
the West end of her said Mothers house, and dryed the
same picture with the fire, and crumbled all the same picture away within a weeke or thereabouts, and about a
weeke

weeke after the Picture was crumbled or mulled away ;
the said *Robinson* dyed.

The reason wherefore shee this Examinate did so
bewitch the said *Robinson* to death, was : for that the said
Robinson had chidden and becalled this Examinate, for
hauing a Bastard-child with one *Seller*.

And this Examinate further saith and confesseth,
that shee did bewitch the said *Iames Robinson* to death,
as in the said *Iennet Deuice* her examination is confessed.

And further shee saith, and confesseth, that shee with
the wife of *Richard Nutter*, and this Examinates said Mother, ioyned altogether, and did bewitch the said *Henrie
Mytton* to death.

The Examination and Euidence of
IENNET DEVICE, *Daughter of the said* ELIZA-
BETH DEVICE, *late Wife of* IOHN DEVICE, *of
the Forrest of Pendle, in the Countie of Lancaster.*

Against
ELIZABETH DEVICE *her Mother, Prisoner at the
Barre vpon her Arraignement and Triall.* viz.

THe said *Iennet Deuice*, being a yong Maide, about the
age of nine yeares, and commanded to stand vp to
giue euidence against her Mother, Prisoner at the Barre :
Her Mother, according to her accustomed manner, out-
ragiously cursing, cryed out against the child in such
fearefull manner, as all the Court did not a little wonder
at her, and so amazed the child, as with weeping teares
shee

shee cryed out vnto my Lord the Iudge, and told him, shee was not able to speake in the presence of her Mother.

This odious Witch was branded with a preposterous marke in Nature, euen from her birth, which was her left eye, standing lower then the other; the one looking downe, the other looking vp, so strangely deformed, as the best that were present in that Honorable assembly, and great Audience, did affirme, they had not often seene the like.

No intreatie, promise of fauour, or other respect, could put her to silence, thinking by this her outragious cursing and threatning of the child, to inforce her to denie that which she had formerly confessed against her Mother, before M. *Nowel*: Forswearing and denying her owne voluntarie confession, which you haue heard, giuen in euidence against her at large, and so for want of further euidence to escape that, which the Iustice of the Law had prouided as a condigne punishment for the innocent bloud shee had spilt, and her wicked and deuillish course of life.

In the end, when no meanes would serue, his Lordship commanded the Prisoner to be taken away, and the Maide to bee set vpon the Table in the presence of the whole Court, who deliuered her euidence in that Honorable assembly, to the Gentlemen of the Iurie of life and death, as followeth. *viz.*

Iennet Deuice, Daughter of *Elizabeth Deuice*, late Wife of *Iohn Deuice*, of the Forrest of Pendle aforesaid Widdow, confesseth and saith, that her said Mother is a Witch, and that this shee knoweth to be true; for, that shee hath seene her Spirit sundrie times come vnto her said Mother in her owne house, called *Malking-Tower*, in the likenesse of a browne Dogge, which shee called *Ball* ; and at one time amongst others, the said *Ball* did aske this Examinates Mother what she would haue him to doe : and this Examinates Mother answered, that she would haue the said *Ball* to helpe her to kill *Iohn Robinson* of *Barley*, alias *Swyre* : by helpe of which said *Ball*, the said *Swyer* was killed by witch-craft accordingly ; and that this Examinates Mother hath continued a Witch for these three or foure yeares last past. And further, this Examinate confesseth, that about a yeare after, this Examinates Mother called for the said *Ball*, who appeared as aforesaid, asking this Examinates Mother what shee would haue done, who said, that shee would haue him to kill *Iames Robinson*, alias *Swyer*, of *Barlow* aforesaid, Brother to the said *Iohn* : whereunto *Ball* answered, hee would doe it ; and about three weekes after, the said *Iames* dyed.

And this Examinate also saith, that one other time shee was present, when her said Mother did call for the *Her Spi-* said *Ball*, who appeared in manner as aforesaid, and asked *rit.* this Examinates Mother what shee would haue him to doe, whereunto this Examinates Mother then said shee would haue him to kill one *Mitton* of the Rough-Lee, whereupon the said *Ball* said, he would doe it ; and so va-nished away, and about three weekes after, the said *Mitton* likewise dyed.

The Examination of IAMES DEVICE,

sonne of the said ELIZABETH DEVICE: *Taken the seuen and twentieth day of of Aprill,* Annoq; Reg. Regis IACOBI Angliæ, &c. Decimo ac Scociæ, xlv.

Before

ROGER NOVVEL *and* NICHOLAS BANESTER, *Esquires, two of his Maiesties Iustices of the Peace, within the said Countie.* viz.

THe said *Iames Deuice* being examined, saith, That he heard his Grand-mother say, about a yeare agoe, That his mother, called *Elizabeth Deuice*, and others, had killed one *Henry Mitton* of the Rough-Lee aforesaid, by Witchcraft. The reason wherefore he was so killed, was for that this Examinates said Grand-mother *Old Demdike*, had asked the said *Mitton* a penny ; and he denying her thereof, thereupon she procured his death, as aforesaid.

And he, this Examinate also saith, That about three yeares ago, this Examinate being in his Grand-mothers house, with his said mother ; there came a thing in shape of a browne dogge, which his mother called *Ball*, who spake to this Examinates mother, in the sight and hearing of this Examinate, and bad her make a Picture of Clay like vnto *Iohn Robinson*, alias *Swyer*, and drie it hard, and then crumble it by little and little ; and as the said Picture should crumble or mull away, so should the said *Io. Robinson* alias *Swyer* his body decay and weare away. And within two or three dayes after, the Picture shall so all be wasted, and mulled away ; so then the said *Iohn Robinson* should die presently. Vpon the agreement be-

twixt

twixt the said dogge and this Examinates mother ; the said dogge suddenly vanished out of this Examinates sight. And the next day, this Examinate saw his said mother take Clay at the West-end of her said house, and make a Picture of it after the said *Robinson*, and brought into her house, and dried it some two dayes : and about two dayes after the drying thereof, this Examinates said mother fell on crumbling the said Picture of Clay, euery day some, for some three weekes together ; and within two dayes after all was crumbled or mulled away, the said *Iohn Robinson* died.

Being demanded by the Court, what answere shee could giue to the particular points of the Euidence against her, for the death of these seuerall persons ; Impudently shee denied them, crying out against her children, and the rest of the Witnesses against her.

But because I haue charged her to be the principall Agent, to procure a solemne meeting at *Malking-Tower* of the Grand-witches, to consult of some speedy course for the deliuerance of her mother, *Old Demdike*, her daughter, and other Witches at Lancaster : the speedie Execution of Master *Couell*, who little suspected or deserued any such practise or villany against him : The blowing vp of the Castle, with diuers other wicked and diuellish practises and murthers ; I shall make it apparant vnto you, by the particular Examinations and Euidence of her owne children, such as were present at the time of their Consultation, together with her owne Examination and Confession, amongst the Records of the Crowne at Lancaster, as hereafter followeth.

The

The voluntary Confeſsion and Examina-

tion of ELIZABETH DEVICE, *taken at the houſe of*
IAMES WILSEY, *of the Forreſt of Pendle, in the*
Countie of Lancaſter, the ſeuen and twentieth day of A-
prill, Annoq; Reg. Regis IACOBI *Angliæ, &c. De-*
cimo, & Scotiæ *Quadrageſimo quinto.*

Before

ROGER NOVVEL *and* NICHOLAS BANISTER,
Eſquires, two of his Maieſties Iuſtices of the Peace within the ſame Countie. viz.

THe said *Elizabeth Deuice* being further Examined,
confeſseth that vpon Good-Friday laſt, there dined
at this Examinates house, called *Malking-Tower,* those
which she hath said are Witches, and doth verily think
them to be Witches : and their names are those whom
Iames Deuice hath formerly spoken of to be there. And
she further saith, that there was also at her said mothers
house, at the day and time aforesaid, two women of
Burneley Parish, whose names the wife of *Richard Nut-*
ter doth know. And there was likewise there one *Anne*
Crouckshey of Marsden : And shee also confeſseth, in all
things touching the Chriſtening of the Spirit, and the
killing of Maſter *Liſter* of Weſtbie, as the said *Iames De-*
uice hath before confessed ; but denieth of any talke was
amongſt them the said Witches, to her now remembrance, at the said meeting together, touching the killing of the Galoer, or the blowing vp of Lancaſter Caſtle.

G 3   *The*

The Examination and Euidence of
IENNET DEVICE, *daughter of the said* ELIZA-
BETH DEVICE, *late wife of* IOHN DEVICE, *of
the Forrest of Pendle, in the Countie of Lancaster.*

Against

ELIZABETH DEVICE, *her Mother, prisoner at the
Barre, vpon her Arraignement and Triall*, viz.

THe said *Iennet Deuice* saith, That vpon Good Friday
last there was about twentie persons (whereof onely two were men, to this Examinates remembrance) at
her said Grandmothers house, called Malking-Tower
aforesaid, about twelue of the clocke : all which persons this Examinates said mother told her, were Witches, and that they came to giue a name to *Alizon Deuice* Spirit, or Familiar, sister to this Examinate, and now
prisoner at Lancaster. And also this Examinate saith,
That the persons aforesaid had to their dinners Beefe,
Bacon, and roasted Mutton ; which Mutton (as this
Examinates said brother said) was of a Wether of *Christopher Swyers* of Barley : which Wether was brought in
the night before into this Examinates mothers house
by the said *Iames Deuice*, this Examinates said brother :
and in this Examinates sight killed and eaten, as aforesaid. And she further saith, That shee knoweth the
names of sixe of the said Witches, *viz.* the wife of *Hugh
Hargraues* vnder Pendle, *Christopher Howgate* of Pendle,
vnckle to this Examinate, and *Elizabeth* his wife, and
Dicke Miles his wife of the Rough-Lee ; *Christopher
Iackes* of Thorny-holme, and his wife : and the names

of the residue shee this Examinate doth not know, sauing that this Examinates mother and brother were both there. And lastly, she this Examinate confesseth and saith, That her mother hath taught her two prayers : the one to cure the bewitched, and the other to get drinke ; both which particularly appeare.

The Examination and Euidence of IAMES DEVICE, *sonne of the said* ELIZABETH DEVICE, *late wife of* IOHN DEVICE, *of the Forrest of Pendle, in the Countie of Lancaster.*

Against
ELIZABETH DEVICE, *his Mother, prisoner at the Barre, vpon her Arraignement and Triall*, viz.

THE said *Iames Deuice* saith, That on Good-Friday last, about twelue of the clocke in the day time, there dined in this Examinates said mothers house, at Malking-Tower, a number of persons, whereof three were men, with this Examinate, and the rest women ; and that they met there for three causes following (as this Examinates said mother told this Examinate) The first was, for the naming of the Spirit, which *Alizon Deuice*, now prisoner at Lancaster, had : But did not name him, because shee was not there. The second was, for the deliuerie of his said Grandmother, olde *Dembdike* ; this Examinates said sister *Allizon* ; the said

Anne

Anne Chattox, and her daughter *Redferne* ; killing the Gaoler at Lancaſter ; and before the next Assises to blow vp the Caſtle there : and to that end the aforesaid prisoners might by that time make an escape, and get away. All which this Examinate then heard them conferre of.

And he also sayth, That the names of the said Witches as were on Good-Friday at this Examinates said Grandmothers house, and now this Examinates owne mothers, for so many of them as hee did know, were these, *viz.* The wife of *Hugh Hargreiues* of Burley ; the wife of *Chriſtopher Bulcock*, of the Mosse end, and *Iohn* her sonne ; the mother of *Myles Nutter* ; *Elizabeth*, the wife of *Chriſtopher Hargreiues*, of Thurniholme ; *Chriſtopher Howgate*, and *Elizabeth*, his wife ; *Alice Graye* of Coulne, and one *Mould-heeles* wife, of the same : and this Examinate, and his Mother. And this Examinate further sayth, That all the Witches went out of the said House in their owne shapes and likenesses. And they all, by that they were forth of the dores, gotten on Horsebacke, like vnto Foales, some of one colour, some of another ; and *Preſtons* wife was the laſt : and when shee got on Horsebacke, they all presently vanished out of this Examinates sight. And before their said parting away, they all appointed to meete at the said *Preſtons* wiues house that day twelue-moneths ; at which time the said *Preſtons* wife promised to make them a great Feaſt. And if they had occasion to meete in the meane time, then should warning be giuen, that they all should meete vpon *Romleyes* Moore.

Executed at Yorks the laſt Aſſiſes.

And

And here they parted, with resolution to execute
their deuillish and bloudie practises, for the deliuerance of their friends, vntill they came to meete here,
where their power and ſtrength was gone. And now
finding her Meanes was gone, shee cryed out for Mercie. Whereupon shee being taken away, the next
in order was her sonne *Iames Deuice*, whom
shee and her Mother, old *Demb-
dike*, brought to act his part
in this wofull Tra-
gedie.

H THE

THE ARRAIGNMENT

and Triall of I A M E S   D E V I C E,
Sonne of Elizabeth Device, *of the Forreſt of Pendle, within the Countie of Lancaſter aforesaid, Laborer, for Witchcraft ; Vpon Tuesday the eighteenth of Auguſt, at the Assises and generall Gaole-Deliuerie holden at Lancaſter*

Before

Sir Edvvard Bromley *Knight, one of his Maieſties Iuſtices of Assise at Lancaſter.*

James Deuice.

THis wicked and miserable Wretch, whether by practise, or meanes, to bring himselfe to some vntimely death, and thereby to auoide his Tryall by his Countrey, and iuſt iudgement of the Law ; or ashamed to bee openly charged with so many deuillish practises, and so much innocent bloud as hee had spilt ; or by reason of his Imprisonment so long time before his Tryall (which was with more fauour, commiseration, and reliefe then hee deserued) I know not : But being brought forth to the

Barre, to receiue his Triall before this worthie Iudge, and so Honourable and Worshipfull an Assembly of Iuſtices for this seruice, was so insensible, weake, and vnable in all thinges, as he could neither speake, heare, or ſtand, but was holden vp when hee was brought to the place of his Arraignment, to receiue his triall.

This *Iames Deuice* of the Forreſt of Pendle, being brought to the Barre, was there according to the forme, order, and course, Indiƈted and Arraigned ; for that hee Felloniously had praƈtised, vsed, and exercised diuers wicked and deuillish Arts, called *Witch-crafts, Inchauntments, Charmes,* and *Sorceries,* in, and vpon one *Anne Towneley,* wife of *Henrie Towneley* of the Carre, in the Countie of Lancaſter Gentleman, and her by force of the same, felloniously had killed. *Contra pacem, &c.*

The said *Iames Deuice* was the second time Indiƈted and Arraigned in the same manner and forme, for the death of *Iohn Duckworth,* by witch-craft. *Contra pacem, &c.*

To these two seuerall Indiƈtments vpon his Arraignment, he pleaded not guiltie, and for the triall of his life put himselfe vpon God and his Countrie.

So as now the Gentlemen of the Iurie of life & death ſtand charged to finde, whether he be guiltie of these, or either of them.

Whereupon Maſter *Nowel* humbly prayed Maſter *Towneley* might be called, who attended to prosecute and giue euidence againſt him for the Kings Majeſtie, and that the particular Examinations taken before him and others, might be openly published & read in Court, in the hearing of the Prisoner.

But

But because it were infinite to bring him to his particular Triall for euery offence, which hee hath committed in his time, and euery practice wherein he hath had
his hand : I shall proceede in order with the Euidence
remayning vpon Record against him, amongst the Records of the Crowne ; both how, and in what sort hee
came to be a witch : and shew you what apparant proofe
there is to charge him with the death of these two feue-
rall persons, for the which hee now standeth vpon his
triall for al the rest of his deuillish practises, incantations,
murders, charmes, sorceries, meetings to consult with
Witches, to execute mischiefe (take them as they are a-
gainst him vpon Record :) Enough, I doubt not. For
these with the course of his life will serue his turne to
deliuer you from the danger of him that neuer tooke
felicitie in any things, but in reuenge, bloud, & mischiefe
with crying out vnto God for vengeance ; which hath
now at the length brought him to the place where hee
standes to receiue his Triall with more honor, fauour,
and respect, then such a Monster in Nature doth de-
serue ; And I doubt not, but in due time by the
Iustice of the Law, to an vntimely
and shamefull
death.

The

The Examination of IAMES DEVICE,

sonne of ELIZABETH DEVICE, *of the Forrest of Pendle, in the Countie of Lancaster, Labourer. Taken the seuen and twentieth day of Aprill, Anno⁴, Reg. Regis* IACOBI, *Angliæ, &c.* x°. *& Scotiæ Quadragesimo quinto.*

Before

ROGER NOWEL, *and* NICHOLAS BANNE-STER, *Esquires : two of his* ᴄMaiesties *Iustices of Peace within the said Countie.*

HE saith, that vpon Sheare Thursday was two yeares, his Grand-Mother *Elizabeth Sothernes*, alias *Dembdike*, did bid him this Examinate goe to the church to receiue the Communion (the next day after being Good Friday) and then not to eate the Bread the Minister gaue him, but to bring it and deliuer it to such a thing as should meet him in his way homewards : Notwithstanding her perswasions, this Examinate did eate the Bread : and so in his comming homeward some fortie roodes off the said Church, there met him a thing in the shape of a Hare, who spoke vnto this Examinate, and asked him whether hee had brought the Bread that his Grand-mother had bidden him, or no? whereupon this Examinate answered, hee had not : and thereupon the said thing threatned to pull this Examinate in peeces, and so this Examinate thereupon marked himselfe to God, and so the said thing vanished out of this Examinates sight. And within some foure daies after that, there appeared in this Examinates sight, hard by the new Church in Pendle, a thing like vnto a browne

Dogge,

Dogge, who asked this Examinate to giue him his Soule, and he should be reuenged of any whom hee would : whereunto this Examinate answered, that his Soule was not his to giue, but was his *Sauiour Iesus Chrifts*, but as much as was in him this Examinate to giue, he was contented he should haue it.

And within two or three daies after, this Examinate went to the Carre-Hall, and vpon some speeches betwixt Miſtris *Towneley* and this Examinate ; Shee charging this Examinate and his said mother, to haue ſtolne some Turues of hers, badde him packe the doores : and withall as he went forth of the doore, the said Miſtris *Towneley* gaue him a knock betweene the shoulders : and about a day or two after that, there appeared vnto this Examinate in his way, a thing like vnto a black dog, who put this Examinate in minde of the said Miſtris *Towneleyes* falling out with him this Examinate ; who bad this Examinate make a Picture of Clay, like vnto the said Miſtris *Towneley* : and that this Examinate with the helpe of his Spirit (who then euer after bidde this Examinate to call it *Dandy*) would kill or deſtroy the said Miſtris *Towneley:* and so the said dogge vanished out of this Examinates sight. And the next morning after, this Examinate tooke Clay, and made a Picture of the said Miſtris *Towneley*, and dried it the same night by the fire : and within a day after, hee, this Examinate began to crumble the said Picture, euery day some, for the space of a weeke : and within two daies after all was crumbled away ; the said Miſtris *Towneley* died.

And hee further saith, That in Lent laſt one *Iohn Duckworth* of the Lawnde, promised this Examinate an old shirt : and within a fortnight after, this Examinate

went

went to the said *Duckworthes* house, and demanded the said old shirt ; but the said *Duckworth* denied him thereof. And going out of the said house, the said Spirit *Dandy* appeared vnto this Examinate, and said, Thou didst touch the said *Duckworth* ; whereunto this Examinate answered, he did not touch him : yes (said the Spirit againe) thou didst touch him, and therefore I haue power of him : whereupon this Examinate ioyned with the said Spirit, and then wished the said Spirit to kill the said *Duckworth* : and within one weeke, then next after, *Duckworth* died.

This voluntary Confession and Examination of his owne, containing in it selfe matter sufficient in Law to charge him, and to proue his offences, contained in the two seuerall Indictments, was sufficient to satisfie the Gentlemen of the Iury of Life and Death, that he is guiltie of them, and either of them : yet my Lord *Bromley* commanded, for their better satisfaction, that the Witnesses present in Court against any of the Prisoners, should be examined openly, *viua voce*, that the Prisoner might both heare and answere to euery particular point of their Euidence ; notwithstanding any of their Examinations taken before any of his Maiesties Iustices of Peace within the same Countie.

Herein do but obserue the wonderfull work of God ; to raise vp a yong Infant, the very sister of the Prisonr, *Iennet Deuice*, to discouer, iustifie and proue these things against him, at the time of his Arraignment and Triall, as hereafter followeth. *viz.*

The

The Examination and Euidence of IEN-
net DEVICE *daughter of* ELIZABETH DEVICE,
late wife of IOHN DEVICE *of of the Forreſt of Pen-*
dle, in the Countie of Lancaſter.

Against
IAMES DEVICE, *Prisoner at the Barre, vpon his Ar-*
raignement and Triall. viz.

BEing examined in open Court, she saith, That her
brother *Iames Deuice*, the Prisoner at the Barre, hath
beene a Witch for the space of three yeares : about the
beginning of which time, there appeared vnto him, in
this Examinates mothers house, a Black-Dogge, which

Dandy. her said brother called *Dandy*. And further, this Examinate confesseth, & saith : That her said brother about
a twelue month since, in the presence of this Examinate,
and in the house aforesaid, called for the said *Dandy*,
who thereupon appeared ; asking this Examinates brother what he would haue him to doe. This Examinates
brother then said, he would haue him to helpe him to
kill old Miſtris *Towneley* of the Carre : whereunto the
said *Dandy* answered, and said, That her said brother
should haue his beſt helpe for the doing of the same ; and
that her said brother, and the said *Dandy*, did both in
this Examinates hearing, say, they would make away
the said Miſtris *Towneley*. And about a weeke after, this
Examinate comming to the Carre-Hall, saw the said
Miſtris *Towneley* in the Kitchin there, nothing well :
whereupon it came into this Examinates minde, that
her said brother, by the help of *Dandy*, had brought the
said Miſtris *Towneley* into the ſtate she then was in.

Which

Which Examinat, although she were but very yong, yet it was wonderfull to the Court, in so great a Presence and Audience, with what modeſtie, gouernement, and vnderſtanding, shee deliuered this Euidence againſt the Prisoner at the Barre, being her owne naturall brother, which he himselfe could not deny, but there acknowledged in euery particular to be iuſt and true.

But behold a little further, for here this bloudy Monſter did not ſtay his hands : for besides his wicked and diuellish Spels, praϲΤises, meetings to consult of murder and mischiefe, which (by Gods grace) hereafter shall follow in order againſt him ; there is yet more bloud to be laid vnto his charge. For although he were but yong, and in the beginning of his Time, yet was he carefull to obserue his InſtruϲΤions from *Old Demdike* his Grandmother, and *Elizabeth Deuice* his mother, in so much that no time should passe since his firſt entrance into that damnable Arte and exercise of Witchcrafts, Inchantments, Charmes and Sorceries, without mischiefe or murder. Neither should any man vpon the leaſt occasion of offence giuen vnto him, escape his hands, without ſome danger. For these particulars were no sooner giuen in Euidence againſt him, when he was againe IndiϲΤed and Arraigned for the murder of these two. *viʒ.*

Iames Deuice of the Forreſt of Pendle aforesaid, in the Countie of Lancaſter, Labourer, the third time IndiϲΤed and Arraigned for the death of *Iohn Hargraues* of Gould-shey-booth, in the Countie of Lancaſter, by Witchcraft, as aforesaid. *Contra &c.*

To this Inditement vpon his Arraignement, he pleaded thereunto not guiltie : and for his Triall put himſelfe vpon God and his Countrey, &c.

I

Iames

Iames Deuice of the Forrest of Pendle aforesaid, in the County of Lancaster, Labourer, the fourth time Indicted and Arraigned for the death of *Blaze Hargreues* of Higham, in the Countie of Lancaster, by Witchcraft, as aforesaid. *Contra Pacem*, &c.

To this Indictment vpon his Arraignement, he pleaded thereunto not guiltie ; and for the Triall of his life, put himselfe vpon God and the Countrey. &c.

Hereupon *Iennet Deuice* produced, sworne and examined, as a witnesse on his Maiesties behalfe, against the said *Iames Deuice*, was examined in open Court, as followeth. *viz.*

The Examination and Euidence of IEN-NET DEVICE *aforesaid.*

Against
IAMES DEVICE, *her brother, Prisoner at the Barre, vpon his Arraignement and Triall.* viz.

BEing sworne and examined in open Court, she saith, That her brother *Iames Deuice* hath beene a Witch for the space of three yeares : about the beginning of which time, there appeared vnto him, in this Examinates mothers house, a Blacke-Dogge, which her said brother called *Dandy*, which *Dandy* did aske her said brother what he would haue him to doe, whereunto he answered, hee would haue him to kill *Iohn Hargreiues*, of Gold-shey-booth : whereunto *Dandy* answered that he would doe it ; since which time the said *Iohn* is dead.

And

And at another time this Examinate confesseth and saith, That her said brother did call the said *Dandy* : who thereupon appeared in the ﹍id house, asking this Examinates brother what hee would haue him to doe : whereupon this Examinates said brother said, he would haue him to kill *Blaze Hargreiues* of Higham : whereupon *Dandy* answered, hee should haue his beſt helpe, and so vanished away : and shee saith, that since that time the said *Hargreiues* is dead ; but how long after, this Examinate doth not now remember.

All which things, when he heard his siſter vpon her Oath affirme, knowing them in his conscience to bee iuſt and true, slenderly denyed them, and thereupon insiſted.

To this Examination were diuerse witnesses examined in open Court *viua voce*, concerning the death of the parties, in such manner and forme, and at such time as the said *Iennet Deuice* in her Euidence hath formerly declared to the Court.

Which is all, and I doubt not but matter sufficient in Law to charge him with, for the death of these parties.

For the proofe of his Praƈtises, Charmes, Meetings at Malking-Tower, to consult with Witches to execute mischiefe, Maſter *Nowel* humbly prayed, his owne Examination, taken and certified, might openly be read ; and the reſt in order, as they remaine vpon Record amongſt the Records of the Crowne at Lancaſter : as hereafter followeth, *viz.*

The

The Examination of IAMES DE-VICE, *Sonne of* ELIZABETH DEVICE, *of the Forrest of Pendle : Taken the seuen and twentieth day of Aprill aforesaid,*

Before

ROGER NOVVEL *and* NICHOLAS BANESTER *Esquires, two of his Maiesties Iustices of Peace within the said Countie,* viz.

ANd being examined, he further saith, That vpon Sheare-Thursday last, in the euening, he this Examinate stole a Wether from *Iohn Robinson* of Barley, and brought it to his Grand-mothers house, old *Dembdike*, and there killed it : and that vpon the day following, being Good-Friday, about twelue of the clocke in the day time, there dined in this Examinates mothers house a number of persons, whereof three were men, with this Examinate, and the rest women ; and that they met there for three Causes following, as this Examinates said Mother told this Examinate.

1   The first was, for the naming of the Spirit which *Alizon Deuice*, now prisoner at Lancaster, had, but did not name him, because she was not there.

2   The second Cause was, for the deliuerie of his said Grand-mother ; this Examinates said sister *Alizon* ; the said *Anne Chattox*, and her daughter *Redferne* ; killing the Gaoler at Lancaster ; and before the next Assises to blow vp the Castle there, to the end the aforesaid persons might by that meanes make an escape & get away : all which this Examinate then heard them conferre of.

3   And the third Cause was, for that there was a wo-

man

man dwelling in Gisborne Parish, who came into this Examinates said Grandmothers house, who there came and craued assistance of the rest of them that were then there, for the killing of Master *Lister* of Westby, because (as shee then said) he had borne malice vnto her, and had thought to haue put her away at the last Assises at Yorke, but could not : and this Examinate heard the said woman say, That her power was not strong ynough to doe it her selfe, being now lesse then before time it had beene.

And also, that the said *Iennet Preston* had a Spirit with her like vnto a white Foale, with a blacke spot in the forhead.

And he also saith, That the names of the said Witches as were on Good-Friday at this Examinates said Grandmothers house, & now this Examinates owne mothers, for so many of them as he did know, were these, *viz.* the wife of *Hugh Hargreiues* of Barley ; the wife of *Christopher Bulcock* of the Mosse end, and *Iohn* her sonne ; the mother of *Myles Nutter* ; *Elizabeth*, the wife of *Christopher Hargreiues*, of Thurniholme ; *Christopher Howgate*, and *Elizabeth* his wife ; *Alice Graye* of Coulne, and one *Mouldheeles* wife, of the same : and this Examinate, and his Mother. And this Examinate further saith, That all the said Witches went out of the said House in their owne shapes and likenesses. And they all, by that they were forth of the dores, were gotten on Horsebacke, like vnto Foales, some of one colour, some of another ; and *Prestons* wife was the last : and when shee got on Horsebacke, they all presently vanished out of this Examinates sight. And before their said parting away, they all appointed to meete at the said *Prestons*

I 3   wiues

wiues house that day twelue-moneths ; at which time
the said *Preſtons* wife promised to make them a great
Feaſt. And if they had occasion to meete in the meane
time, then should warning be giuen, that they all should
meete vpon *Romleyes* Moore.

The Examination and Euidence of
IENNET DEVICE.

Againſt

IAMES DEVICE *her said Brother, Prisoner at the
Barre, vpon his Arraignement and Triall : Taken before*
ROGER NOWEL, *and* NICHOLAS BANNE-
STER, *Esquires : two of his eMaieſties Iuſtices of Peace
within the said Countie.* viz.

SHee saith, that vpon Good-Friday laſt there was a-
bout twentie persons, whereof only two were men,
to this Examinates remembrance, at her said Grand-
mothers house, called *eMalking-Tower* aforesaid, about
twelue of the clock : all which persons this Examinates
said Mother told her were Witches, and that they came
to giue a name to *Alizon Deuice* Spirit or Familiar, Siſter
to this Examinate, and now Prisoner, in the Caſtle of
Lancaſter : And also this Examinate saith, that the persons aforesaid had to their Dinners, Beefe, Bacon, and
roſted Mutton, which Mutton, as this Examinates said
brother said, was of a Weather of *Robinsons* of Barley :
which Weather was brought in the night before into
this Examinates mothers house, by the said *Iames Deuice*

this Examinates said brother, and in this Examinates sight killed, and eaten, as aforesaid : And shee further saith, that shee knoweth the names of sixe of the said Witches, *viz.* the wife of the said *Hugh Hargreiues*, vnder Pendle : *Chriſtopher Howget*, of Pendle, Vncle to this Examinate : and *Dick Miles* wife, of the Rough-Lee : *Chriſtopher Iacks*, of Thorne-holme, and his Wife : and the names of the residue shee this Examinate doth not know, sauing that this Examinates Mother and Brother were both there.

The Examination of ELIZABETH

DEVICE, *Mother of the said* IAMES DEVICE, *of the Forreſt of Pendle : taken the seuen and twentieth day of Aprill aforesaid.*

Before

ROGER NOWEL, *and* NICHOLAS BANNE-STER, *Esquires ; as aforesaid.* viz.

BEing examined, the said *Elizabeth* saith and confesseth, that vpon Good-Friday laſt there dined at this Examinates house, those which she hath said to be Witches, and doth verily thinke them to bee Witches, and their names are those, whom *Iames Deuice* hath formerly spoken of to be there.

And shee also confesseth in all things touching the Chriſtning of her Spirit, and the killing of Maſter *Liſter* of Weſtby, as the said *Iames Deuice* confesseth. But denieth that any talke was amongſt the thē said Witches, to her now remembrance, at the said meeting together, tou-

touching the killing of the Gaoler at Lancaſter; blowing vp of the Castle, thereby to deliuer old *Dembdike* her Mother; *Alizon Deuice* her Daughter, and other Priſoners, committed to the said Caſtle for Witchcraft.

> After all these things opened, and deliuered in euidence againſt him; Maſter *Couil*, who hath the cuſtodie of the Gaole at Lancaſter, hauing taken great paines with him during the time of his impriſonment, to procure him to discouer his pra-ctizes, and such other Witches as he knew to bee dangerous: Humbly prayed the fauour of the Court, that his voluntarie confession to M. *Anderton*, M. *Sands* the Major of Lancaſter, M. *Couel*, and others, might openly bee published and declared in Court.

---

*The voluntarie confession and declara-*tion *of* IAMES DEVICE, *Prisoner in the Caſtle at Lan-caſter.*

Before

WILLIAM SANDS, *Maior of Lancaſter,* IAMES ANDERTON, *Esquire, one of his Maieſties Iuſtices of Peace within the Countie of Lancaſter: And* THOMAS COVEL, *Gentleman, one of his Maieſties Coroners in the same Countie.* viz.

I Ames *Deuice*, Prisoner in the Caſtle at Lancaſter, saith; That his said Spirit *Dandie*, being very earneſt with him

him to giue him his soule, He answered, he would giue him that part thereof that was his owne to giue : and thereupon the said Spirit said, hee was aboue C H R I S T I E S V S, and therefore hee must absolutely giue him his Soule : and that done, hee would giue him power to re-uenge himselfe against any whom he disliked.

And he further saith, that the said Spirit did appeare vnto him after sundrie times, in the likenesse of a Dogge, and at euery time most earnestly perswaded him to giue him his Soule absolutely : who answered as before, that he would giue him his owne part and no further. And hee saith, that at the last time that the said Spirit was with him, which was the Tuesday next before his ap-prehension, when as hee could not preuaile with him to haue his Soule absolutely granted vnto him, as afore-said ; the said Spirit departed from him, then giuing a most fearefull crie and yell, and withall caused a great flash of fire to shew about him : which said Spirit did neuer after trouble this Examinate.

William Sands,
James Anderton.
Tho. Couel, Coroner.

The said *Iennet Deuice,* his Sister, in the very end of her Examination against the said *Iames Deuice,* confes-seth and saith, that her Mother taught her two Prayers : the one to get drinke, which was this. *viz.*

Crucifixus hoc signum vitam
Eternam. Amen.

And

And shee further saith, That her Brother *Iames De-uice*, the Prisoner at the Barre, hath confessed to her this Examinate, that he by this Prayer hath gotten drinke : and that within an houre after the saying the said Prayer, drinke hath come into the house after a very strange manner. And the other Prayer, the said *Iames Deuice* affirmed, would cure one bewitched, which shee recited as followeth. *viz.*

A Charme.

Vpon Good-Friday, I will fast while I may
Vntill I heare them knell
Our Lords owne Bell,
Lord in his messe
With his twelue Apostles good,
What hath he in his hand
Ligh in leath wand :
What hath he in his other hand ?
Heauens doore key,
Open, open Heauen doore keyes,
Steck, steck hell doore.
Let Crizum child
Goe to it Mother mild,
What is yonder that casts a light so farrandly,
Mine owne deare Sonne that's naild to the Tree.
He is naild sore by the heart and hand,
And holy barne Panne,
Well is that man
That Fryday spell can,
His Childe to learne ;
A Crosse of Blew, and another of Red,

As

As good Lord was to the Roode.
Gabriel *laid him downe to sleepe*
Vpon the ground of holy weepe :
Good Lord came walking by,
Sleep'ſt thou, wak'ſt thou Gabriel,
No Lord I am ſled with ſlicke and ſlake,
That I can neither sleepe nor wake :
Rise vp Gabriel *and goe with me,*
The ſlick nor the ſlake shall neuer deere thee.
Sweete Ieſus our Lord, Amen.

Iames Deuice.

What can be said more of this painfull Steward, that
was so carefull to prouide Mutton againſt this Feaſt and
solemne meeting at *Malking-Tower,* of these hellish and
diuellish band of Witches, (the like whereof hath not
been heard of) then hath beene openly published and
declared againſt him at the Barre, vpon his Arraignement and Triall : wherein it pleased God to raise vp
Witnesses beyond expectation to conuince him ; besides
his owne particular Examinations, which being shewed
and read vnto him; he acknowledged to be iuſt and true.
And what I promised to set forth againſt him, in the beginning of his Arraignment and Triall, I doubt not but
therein I haue satisfied your expectation at large,
wherein I haue beene very sparing to charge him with
any thing, but with sufficient matter of Record and E-
uidence, able to satisfie the consciences of the Gentlemen of the Iury of Life and Death ; to whose good consideration I leaue him, with the perpetuall Badge and
Brand of as dangerous and malicious a Witch, as euer
liued in these parts of Lancashire, of his time : and spot-

K 2   ted

ted with as much Innocent bloud, as euer any Witch of
his yeares.

After all these proceedings, by direction of his Lordship, were their seuerall Examinations, subscribed by e-
uery one of them in particular, shewed vnto them at the
time of their Triall, & acknowledged by thē to be true,
deliuered to the gentlemen of the Iury of Life & Death,
for the better satisfaction of their consciences : after due
consideration of which said seuerall examinations, confessions, and voluntary declarations, as well of themselues as of their children, friends and confederates, The
Gentlemen deliuered vp their Verdict against the Prisoners, as followeth, *viz.*

The Verdict of Life and Death.

WHo found *Anne Whittle,* alias *Chattox, Elizabeth
Deuice,* and *Iames Deuice,* guiltie of the seuerall
murthers by Witchcraft, contained in the Indictments
against them, and euery of them.

THE

THE WITCHES OF
SALMESBVRY.

The Arraignement and Triall of IEN-
NET BIERLEY ELLEN BIERLEY, *and* IANE
SOVTHVVORTH *of Salmesbury, in the County of
Lancaſter ; for Witchcraft vpon the bodie of* GRACE
SOVVERBVTTS, *vpon Wednesday the nineteenth of
cAuguſt* : *At the cAssises and generall Gaole-deliuery,
holden at Lancaſter.*

Before
Sir EDVVARD BROMLEY *Knight, one of hù Maieſtices Iuſtices of Assiʒe at Lancaſter* : *as hereafter followeth.* viz.

Iennet Bierley.
Ellen Bierley.
Iane Southworth.

Hus haue we for a time left the Graund
Witches of the Forreſt of Pendle, to the
good consideration of a verie sufficient
Iury of worthy Gentlemen of their Coũ-
trey. We are now come to the famous
Witches of Salmesbury, as the Countrey called them,
K 3   who

who by such a subtill practise and conspiracie of a Seminarie Priest, or, as the best in this Honorable Assembly thinke, a Iesuite, whereof this Countie of Lancaster hath good store, who by reason of the generall entertainement they find, and great maintenance they haue, resort hither, being farre from the Eye of Iustice, and therefore, *Procul a fulmine* ;   are now brought to the Barre, to receiue their Triall, and such a young witnesse prepared and instructed to giue Euidence against them, that it must be the Act of G o d that must be the means to discouer their Practises and Murthers, and by an infant : but how and in what sort Almightie G o d deliuered them from the stroake of Death, when the Axe was layd to the Tree, and made frustrate the practise of this bloudie Butcher, it shall appeare vnto you vpon their Arraignement and Triall, whereunto they are now come.

Master *Thomas Couel*, who hath the charge of the prisoners in the Castle at Lancaster, was commaunded to bring forth the said

Jennet Bierley,
Ellen Bierley,
Jane Southworth,

to the Barre to receiue their Triall.

Indictment.

THe said *Iennet Bierley*, *Ellen Bierly*, and *Iane Southworth* of Salmesbury, in the Countie of Lancaster,
be-

being indicted, for that they and euery of them felloniously had practised, exercised, and used diuerse deuillish
and wicked Arts, called *Witchcrafts, Inchauntments,*
Charmes, and *Sorceries,* in and vpon one *Grace Sowerbuts :*
so that by meanes thereof her bodie wasted and consumed, *Contra formam Statuti &c. Et Contra Pacem dicti*
Domini Regis Coronam & dignitatem &c.

To this Indictment vpon their Arraignement, they
pleaded *Not-Guiltie* ; and for the Triall of their liues put
themselues vpon G o d and their Countrey.

Whereupon Master Sheriffe of the Countie of Lancaster, by direction of the Court, made returne of a very
sufficient Iurie to passe betweene the Kings Maiestie
and them, vpon their liues and deaths, with such others
as follow in order.

The Prisoners being now at the Barre vpon their
Triall, *Grace Sowerbutts,* the daughter of *Thomas Sower-*
butts, about the age of foureteene yeares, was produced to giue Euidence for the Kings Maiestie against
them : who standing vp, she was commaunded to point out the Prisoners, which
shee did, and said as followeth, *viz.*

⁂

The Examination and Euidence of

G R A C E   S O V V E R B V T T S, *daughter of* T H O M A S
S O V V E R B V T T S, *of Salmesbury, in the Countie of
Lancaster Husband-man, vpon her Oath,*

Against

I E N N E T   B I E R L E Y,   E L L E N   B I E R L E Y,   *and*
I A N E   S O V T H V V O R T H, *prisoners at the Barre, vpon
their Arraignement and Triall,* viz.

THe said *Grace Sowerbutts* vpon her oath saith, That
for the space of some yeares now last past shee hath
beene haunted and vexed with some women, who haue
vsed to come to her : which women, shee sayth, were
Iennet Bierley, this Informers Grand-mother ; *Ellen Bierley*, wife to *Henry Bierley* ; *Iane Southworth*, late the wife
of *Iohn Southworth*, and one *Old Doewife*, all of Salmesburie aforesaid. And shee saith, That now lately those
foure women did violently draw her by the haire of the
head, and layd her on the toppe of a Hay-mowe, in
the said *Henry Bierleyes* Barne. And shee saith further,
That not long after the said *Iennet Bierley* did meete
this Examinate neere vnto the place where shee dwelleth, and first appeared in her owne likenesse, and after
that in the likenesse of a blacke Dogge, and as this Examinate did goe ouer a Style, shee picked her off : how-
beit shee saith shee had no hurt then, but rose againe,
and went to her Aunts in Osbaldeston, and returned
backe againe to her Fathers house the same night, being fetched home by her father. And she saith, That
in her way home-wards shee did then tell her Father,
how

how shee had beene dealt withall both then and at sundry times before that; and before that time she neuer
told any bodie thereof: and being examined why she
did not, she sayth, she could not speake thereof, though
she desired so to doe. And she further sayth, That vpon Saterday, being the fourth of this inſtant Aprill,
shee this Examinate going towards Salmesbury bote,
to meete her mother, comming from Preſton, shee saw
the said *Iennet Bierley*, who met this Examinate at a
place called the Two Brigges, firſt in her owne shape,
and afterwards in the likenesse of a blacke Dogge, with
two legges, which Dogge went close by the left side of
this Examinate, till they came to a Pitte of Water, and
then the said Dogge spake, and persuaded this Examinate to drowne her selfe there, saying, it was a faire and
an easie death: Whereupon this Examinate thought
there came one to her in a white sheete, and carried
her away from the said Pitte, vpon the comming
whereof the said blacke Dogge departed away; and
shortly after the said white thing departed also: And
after this Examinate had gone further on her way, a-
bout the length of two or three Fields, the said blacke
Dogge did meete her againe, and going on her left side,
as aforesaid, did carrie her into a Barne of one *Hugh
Walshmans*, neere there by, and layed her vpon the
Barne-floore, and couered this Examinate with Straw
on her bodie, and Haye on her head, and the Dogge
it selfe lay on the toppe of the said Straw, but how
long the said Dogge lay there, this Examinate cannot
tell, nor how long her selfe lay there: for shee sayth,
That vpon her lying downe there, as aforesaid, her
Speech and Senses were taken from her: and the firſt

L   time

time shee knew where shee was, shee was layed vpon a
bedde in the said *Walshmans* house, which (as shee hath
since beene told) was vpon the Monday at night following : and shee was also told, That shee was found
and taken from the place where shee first lay, by some
of her friends, and carried into the said *Walshmans*
house, within a few houres after shee was layed in the
Barne, as aforesaid. And shee further sayth, That vpon
the day following, being Tuesday, neere night of the
same day, shee this Examinate was fetched by her Father and Mother from the said *Walshmans* house to her
Fathers house. And shee saith, That at the place before specified, called the Two Brigges, the said *Iennet
Bierley* and *Ellen Bierley* did appeare vnto her in their
owne shapes : whereupon this Examinate fell downe,
and after that was not able to speake, or goe, till the Friday following : during which time, as she lay in her Fathers house, the said *Iennet Bierley* and *Ellen Bierley* did
once appeare vnto her in their owne shapes, but they
did nothing vnto her then, neither did shee euer see
them since. And shee further sayth, That a good
while before all this, this Examinate did goe with the
said *Iennet Bierley*, her Grand-mother, and the said
Ellen Bierley her Aunt, at the bidding of her said
Grand-mother, to the house of one *Thomas Walshman*, in Salmesbury aforesaid. And comming thither in the night, when all the house-hold was a-
bed, the doores being shut, the said *Iennet Bierley*
did open them, but this Examinate knoweth not
how : and being come into the said house, this
Examinate and the said *Ellen Bierley* stayed there,
and the said *Iennet Bierley* went into the Chamber

where the said *Walshman* and his wife lay, & from thence
brought a little child, which this Examinate thinketh
was in bed with it Father and Mother : and after the said
Iennet Bierley had set her downe by the fire, with the
said child, shee did thrust a naile into the nauell of the
said child : and afterwards did take a pen and put it in at
the said place, and did suck there a good space, and afterwards laid the child in bed againe : and then the said
Iennet and the said *Ellen* returned to their owne houses,
and this Examinate with them. And shee thinketh that
neither the said *Thomas Walshman*, nor his wife knew that
the said child was taken out of the bed from them. And
shee saith also, that the said child did not crie when it
was hurt, as aforesaid : But she saith, that shee thinketh
that the said child did thenceforth languish, and not
long after dyed. And after the death of the said child ;
the next night after the buriall thereof, the said *Iennet
Bierley & Ellen Bierley*, taking this Examinate with them,
went to Salmesburie Church, and there did take vp the
said child, and the said *Iennet* did carrie it out of the
Church-yard in her armes, and then did put it in her lap
and carryed it home to her owne house, and hauing it
there did boile some therof in a Pot, and some did broile
on the coales, of both which the said *Iennet* and *Ellen* did
eate, and would haue had this Examinate and one *Grace
Bierley*, Daughter of the said *Ellen*, to haue eaten with
them, but they refused so to doe : And afterwards the
said *Iennet & Ellen* did seethe the bones of the said child
in a pot, & with the Fat that came out of the said bones,
they said they would annoint themselues, that thereby
they might sometimes change themselues into other
shapes. And after all this being done, they said they

L 2   would

would lay the bones againe in the graue the next night following, but whether they did so or not, this Examinate knoweth not : Neither doth shee know how they got it out of the graue at the first taking of it vp. And being further sworne and examined, she deposeth & saith, that about halfe a yeare agoe, the said *Iennet Bierley, Ellen Bierley, Iane Southworth,* and this Examinate (who went by the appointment of the said *Iennet* her Grand mother) did meete at a place called Red banck, vpon the North side of the water of Ribble, euery Thursday and Sonday at night by the space of a fortnight, and at the water side there came vnto them, as they went thether, foure black things, going vpright, and yet not like men in the face : which foure did carrie the said three women and this Examinate ouer the Water, and when they came to the said Red Banck, they found some thing there which they did eate. But this Examinate saith, shee neuer saw such meate ; and therefore shee durst not eate thereof, although her said Grand mother did bidde her eate. And after they had eaten, the said three Women and this Examinate danced, euery one of them with one of the black things aforesaid, and after their dancing the said black things did pull downe the said three Women, and did abuse their bodies, as this Examinate thinketh, for shee saith, that the black thing that was with her, did abuse her bodie.

The said Examinate further saith vpon her Oth, That about ten dayes after her Examination taken at Blackborne, shee this Examinate being then come to her Fathers house againe, after shee had beene certaine dayes at her Vnckles house in Houghton : *Iane Southworth* widow, did meet this Examinate at her Fathers house dore

and

and did carrie her into the loft, and there did lay her vp-
pon the floore, where shee was shortly found by her Father and brought downe, and laid in a bed, as afterwards
shee was told : for shee saith, that from the firſt meeting
of the said *Iane Southworth*, shee this Examinate had her
speech and senses taken from her. But the next day shee
saith, shee came somewhat to her selfe, and then the said
Widow *Southworth* came againe to this Examinate to
her bed-side, and tooke her out of bed, and said to this
Examinate, that shee did her no harme the other time,
in respeƈt of that shee now would after doe to her, and
thereupon put her vpon a hey-ſtack, ſtanding some three
or foure yards high from the earth, where shee was
found after great search made, by a neighbours Wife
neare dwelling, and then laid in her bed againe, where
she remained speechlesse and senselesse as before, by the
space of two or three daies : And being recouered, within a weeke after shee saith, that the said *Iane Southworth*
did come againe to this Examinate at her fathers house
and did take her away, and laid her in a ditch neare to
the house vpon her face, and left her there, where shee
was found shortly after, and laid vpon a bedde, but had
not her senses againe of a day & a night, or thereabouts.
And shee further saith, that vpon Tuesday laſt before
the taking of this her Examination, the said *Iane South-*
worth came to this Examinates Fathers house, and finding this Examinate without the doore, tooke her and
carried her into the Barne, and thruſt her head amongſt
a companie of boords that were there ſtanding, where
shee was shortly after found and laid in a bedde, and remained in her old fit till the Thursday at night following.

And being further examined touching her being at
Red-bancke, shee saith, That the three women, by her
before named, were carried backe againe ouer Ribble,
by the same blacke things that carried them thither; and
saith that at their said meeting in the Red-bancke, there
did come also diuers other women, and did meete them
there, some old, some yong, which this Examinate thinketh did dwell vpon the North-side of Ribble, because
she saw them not come ouer the Water: but this Examinate knew none of them, neither did she see them eat
or dance, or doe any thing else that the rest did, sauing
that they were there and looked on.

These particular points of Euidence being thus vr-
ged against the Prisoners: the father of this *Grace Sowerbutts* prayed that *Thomas Walshman*, whose childe they
are charged to murther, might be examined as a witnes
vpon his oath, for the Kings Maiestie, against the Prisoners at the Barre: who vpon this strange deuised accusation, deliuered by this impudent wench, were in opinion of many of that great Audience guilty of this bloudie murther, and more worthy to die than any of these
Witches.

The

The Examination and Euidence of

THOMAS WALSHMAN, *of Salmesbury, in the Countie of Lancaster, Yeoman.*

Against

IENNET BIERLEY, ELLEN BIERLEY, *and* IANE SOVTHVVORTH, *Prisoners at the Barre, vpon their Arraignement and Triall, as followeth.* viz.

THe said Examinate, *Thomas Walshman,* vpon his oath saith, That hee had a childe died about Lent was twelue-month, who had beene sicke by the space of a fortnight or three weekes, and was afterwards buried in Salmesburie Church : which childe when it died was about a yeare old; But how it came to the death of it, this Examinate knoweth not. And he further saith, that about the fifteenth of Aprill last, or thereabouts, the said *Grace Sowerbutts* was found in this Examinates fathers Barne, laid vnder a little hay and straw, and from thence was carried into this Examinates house, and there laid till the Monday at night following : during which time shee did not speak, but lay as if she had beene dead.

The

The Examination of IOHN SINGLE-TON:

Taken at Salmesbury, in the Countie of Lancaster, the seuenth day of August : Anno Reg. Regis IACOBI Angliæ, Franciæ, & Hiberniæ, Fidei Defensor. &c. Decimo & Scotiæ, xlvj.

Before

ROBERT HOVLDEN, *Esquire, one of his Maiesties Iustices of Peace in the County of Lancaster.*

Against

IENNET BIERLEY, ELLEN BIERLEY, *and* IANE SOVTHVVORTH, *which hereafter followeth.*

THe said Examinate vpon his oath saith, That hee hath often heard his old Master, Sir *Iohn Southworth* Knight, now deceased, say, touching the late wife of *Iohn Southworth,* now in the Gaole, for suspition of Witchcraft : That the said wife was as he thought an euill woman, and a Witch : and he said that he was sorry for her husband, that was his kinsman, for he thought she would kill him. And this Examinate further saith, That the said Sir *Iohn Southworth* in his comming or going betweene his owne house at Salmesbury, and the Towne of Preston, did for the most part forbeare to passe by the house, where the said wife dwelled, though it was his nearest and best way ; and rode another way, only for feare of the said wife, as this Examinate verily thinketh.

The

The Examination of WILLIAM

ALKER *of Salmesbury, in the Countie of Lancaster,*
Yeoman : Taken the fifteenth day of Aprill, Anno Reg.
Regis IACOBI, Angliæ, Franciæ, & Hiberniæ, Deci-
mo & Scotiæ, quadragesimo quinto.

Before

ROBERT HOVLDEN, *one of his Maiesties Iustices*
of Peace in the County of Lancaster : *Against* IENNET
BIERLEY, ELLEN BIERLEY, *and* IANE BIER-
LEY, *which hereafter followeth.* viz.

THe said Examinate vpon his oath saith, That hee
hath seene the said Sir *Iohn Southworth* shunne to
meet the said wife of *Iohn Southworth*, now Prisoner in
the Gaole, when he came neere where she was. And hath
heard the said Sir *Iohn Southworth* say, that he liked her
not, and that he doubted she would bewitch him.

Here was likewise *Thomas Sowerbutts*, father of *Grace*
Sowerbutts, examined vpon his oath, and many other
witnesses to little purpose : who being examined by the
Court, could depose little against them : But the finding
of the wench vpon the hay in her counterfeit fits : wher-
fore I leaue to trouble you with the particular declaration of their Euidence against the Prisoners, In respect
there was not any one witnes able to charge them with
one direct matter of Witchcraft ; nor proue any thing
for the murther of the childe.

Herein, before we come to the particular declaration
of that wicked and damnable practise of this Iesuite or
Seminary. I shall commend vnto your examination and
iudgement some points of her Euidence, wherein you

shall

shal see what impossibilities are in this accusatiõ brought
to this perfection, by the great care and paines of this
officious Doctor, Master *Tompson* or *Southworth*, who
commonly worketh vpon the Feminine disposition,
being more Passiue then Actiue.

The particular points of the Euidence of GRACE SOVVERBVTTS, *viz.*

Euidence.

THat *for the space of some yeares she hath been haunted
and vexed with some women, who haue vsed to come
to her.*

The Iesuite forgot to instruct his Scholler how long
it is since she was tormented: it seemes it is long since he
read the old Badge of a Lyer, *Oportet mendacem esse me-
morem.* He knowes not how long it is since they came to
church, after which time they began to practise Witchcraft. It is a likely thing the Torment and Panges of
Witchcraft can be forgotten; and therefore no time can
be set downe.

*Shee saith that now lately these foure women did violently
draw her by the haire of the head, and lay her on the top
of a Hay-mow.*

Heere they vse great violence to her, whome in another place they make a noise to be of their counsell, to go
with them to the house of *Walshman* to murther the
childe. This courtesie deserues no discouery of so foule
a Fact.

Not

Not long after, the said Iennet Bierley *did meet this
Examinate neere vnto the place where she dwelled,
and first appeared in her owne likenesse, and after
that in the likenesse of a blacke Dogge.*

Vno & eodem tempore, shee transformed her selfe into
a Dogge. I would know by what meanes any Priest can
maintaine this point of Euidence.

*And as shee went ouer a Style, shee picked her ouer,
but had no hurt.*

This is as likely to be true as the rest, to throw a
child downe from the toppe of a House, and neuer
hurt her great toe.

*She rose againe ; had no hurt, went to her Aunt,
and returned backe againe to her Fathers house,
being fetched home.*

I pray you obserue these contrarieties, in order as
they are placed, to accuse the Prisoners.

Saterday the fourth of this instant Aprill.

Which was about the very day the Witches of the
Forrest of Pendle were sent to Lancaster. Now was
the time for the Seminarie to instruct, accuse, and call
into question these poore women: for the wrinckles of
an old wiues face is good euidence to the Iurie against
a Witch. And how often will the common people say
(*Her eyes are sunke in her head,* G O D *blesse vs from her.*)
But old *Chattox* had *Fancie,* besides her withered face,
to accuse her.

This

> *This Examinate did goe with the said* Iennet Bier-
> ley *her Grand-mother, and* Ellen Bierley *her
> Aunt, to the house of* Walshman, *in the night-
> time, to murther a Child in a strange manner.*

This of all the rest is impossible, to make her of their
counsell, to doe murther, whome so cruelly and barbarously they pursue from day to day, and torment her.
The Witches of the Forrest of Pendle were neuer so
cruell nor barbarous.

> *And she also saith, the Child cried not when it was
> hurt.*

All this time the Child was asleepe, or the Child was
of an extraordinarie patience, *ô inauditum facinus !*

> *After they had eaten, the said three women and this
> Examinate daunced euery one of them with one of
> the Blacke things : and after, the Blacke things a-
> bused the said women.*

Here is good Euidence to take away their liues. This
is more proper for the Legend of Lyes, then the Euidence of a witnesse vpon Oath, before a reuerend and
learned Iudge, able to conceiue this Villanie, and finde
out the practise. Here is the Religious act of a Priest,
but behold the euent of it.

> *Shee describes the foure Blacke things to goe vpright,
> but not like Men in the face.*

The Seminarie mistakes the face for the feete: For
Chattox and all her fellow Witches agree, the Deuill is
clouen-footed: but *Fancie* had a very good face, and
was a very proper Man.

About

*About tenne dayes after her Examination taken at
Black-borne, then she was tormented.*

Still he pursues his Proiect : for hearing his Scholler
had done well, he laboured she might doe more in this
nature. But notwithstanding, many things are layd to
be in the times when they were Papists : yet the Priest
neuer tooke paines to discouer them, nor instruct his
Scholler, vntill they came to Church. Then all this
was the Act of G o d, to raise a child to open all things,
and then to discouer his plotted Tragedie. Yet in this
great discouerie, the Seminarie forgot to deuise a Spirit
for them.

And for *Thomas Walshman*, vpon his Oath he sayth,
That his Child had beene sicke by the space of a fortnight, or three weekes, before it died. And *Grace Sowerbutts* saith, they tooke it out of the bedde, strucke a nayle
into the Nauell, sucked bloud, layd it downe againe ; and
after, tooke it out of the Graue, with all the rest, as you
haue heard. How these two agree, you may, vpon
view of their Euidence, the better conceiue, and be able
to judge.

How well this proiect, to take away the liues of three
innocent poore creatures by practise and villanie ; to induce a young Scholler to commit periurie, to accuse her
owne Grand-mother, Aunt, &c. agrees either with the
Title of a Iesuite, or the dutie of a Religious Priest, who
should rather professe Sinceritie and Innocencie, then
practise Trecherie : But this was lawfull ; for they are
Heretikes accursed, to leaue the companie of Priests ; to
frequent Churches, heare the word of G o d preached,
and professe Religion sincerely.

M 3   But

But by the course of Times and Accidents, wise men obserue, that very seldome hath any mischieuous attempt beene vnder-taken without the direction or assistance of a Iesuit, or Seminarie Priest.

Who did not condemne these Women vpon this euidence, and hold them guiltie of this so foule and horrible murder? But Almightie God, who in his prouidence had prouided meanes for their deliuerance, although the Priest by the helpe of the Deuill, had prouided false witnesses to accuse them ; yet G o d had prepared and placed in the Seate of Iustice, an vpright Iudge to sit in Iudgement vpon their liues, who after he had heard all the euidence at large against the Prisoners for the Kings Majestie, demanded of them what answere they could make. They humbly vpon their knees with weeping teares, desired him for Gods cause to examine *Grace Sowerbuts*, who set her on, or by whose meanes this accusation came against them.

Immediately the countenance of this *Grace Sowerbuts* changed : The witnesses being behinde, began to quarrell and accuse one an other. In the end his Lordship examined the Girle, who could not for her life make any direct answere, but strangely amazed, told him, shee was put to a Master to learne, but he told her nothing of this.

But here as his Lordships care and paines was great to discouer the practises of these odious Witches of the Forrest of Pendle, and other places, now vpon their triall before him : So was he desirous to discouer this damnable practise, to accuse these poore Women, and bring their liues in danger, and thereby to deliuer the innocent.

And

And as he openly deliuered it vpon the Bench, in the hearing of this great Audience : That if a Priest or Iesuit had a hand in one end of it, there would appeare to bee knauerie, and practise in the other end of it. And that it might the better appeare to the whole World, examined *Thomas Sowerbuts*, what Master taught his daughter : in generall termes, he denyed all.

The Wench had nothing to say, but her Master told her nothing of this. In the end, some that were present told his Lordship the truth, and the Prisoners informed him how shee went to learne with one *Thompson* a Seminarie Priest, who had instructed and taught her this accusation against them, because they were once obstinate Papists, and now came to Church. Here is the discouerie of this Priest, and of his whole practise. Still this fire encreased more and more, and one witnesse accusing an other, all things were laid open at large.

In the end his Lordship tooke away the Girle from her Father, and committed her to M. *Leigh*, a very religious Preacher, and M. *Chisnal*, two Iustices of the Peace, to be carefully examined. Who tooke great paines to examine her of euery particular point : In the end they came into the Court, and there deliuered this Examination as followeth.

⁎

The

The Examination *of* GRACE SOWER-

BVTS, *of Salmesburie, in the Countie of Lancaster, Spin-*
ster : Taken vpon Wednesday the 19. *of* August 1612.
Anno{ Reg. Regis, IACOBI Angliæ, Franciæ, & Hiberniæ, Fidei Defensoris, &c. decimo & Scotiæ, xlvi.

Before

WILLIAM LEIGH, *and* EDWARD CHISNAL,
Esquires ; two of his Maiesties Iustices of Peace in the same
Countie : At the Assizes and generall Gaole deliuerie, hol-
den at Lancaster.

By

Direction of Sir EDWARD BROMLEY *Knight, one*
of his Maiesties *Iustices of Assize at Lancaster.*

BEing demanded whether the accusation shee laid vp-
pon her Grand-mother, *Iennet Bierley, Ellen Bierley,*
and *Iane Southworth,* of Witchcraft, *viz.* of the killing of
the child of *Thomas Walshman,* with a naile in the Nauell,
the boyling, eating, and oyling, thereby to transforme
themselues into diuers shapes, was true ; she doth vt-
terly denie the same ; or that euer shee saw any such practises done by them.

Shee further saith, that one Master *Thompson,* which
she taketh to be Master *Christopher Southworth,* to whom
shee was sent to learne her prayers, did perswade, counsell, and aduise her, to deale as formerly hath beene said
against her said Grand-mother, Aunt, and *Southworths*
wife.

And

And further shee confesseth and saith, that shee neuer did know, or saw any Deuils, nor any other Visi-
ons, as formerly by her hath beene alleaged and informed.

Also shee confesseth and saith, That she was not
throwne or caſt vpon the Henne-ruffe, and Hay-mow
in the Barne, but that shee went vp vpon the Mow her
selfe by the wall side.

Being further demanded whether shee euer was at
the Church, shee saith, shee was not, but promised her after to goe to the Church,
and that very wil-
lingly.

Signum, ✠ Grace Sowerbuts.

William Leigh.

Edward Chisnal.

The Examination of IENNET BIER-LEY, ELLEN BIERLEY, *and* IANE SOVTH-WORTH, *of Salmesburie, in the Countie of Lancaster, Taken vpon Wednesday the nineteenth of August* 1612. *Annoq̔, Reg. Regis,* IACOBI *Angliæ, Franciæ, &* Hiberniæ, *Fidei Defensoris, &c. decimo &* Scotiæ, xlvi.

Before

WILLIAM LEIGH, *and* EDWARD CHISNAL, *Esquires ; two of his Maiesties Iustices of Peace in the same Countie : At the Assizes and generall Gaole deliuerie, holden at Lancaster.*

By

Direction of Sir EDWARD BROMLEY *Knight, one of his Maiesties Iustices of Assize at Lancaster.*

IEnnet Bierley being demanded what shee knoweth, or hath heard, how *Grace Sowerbuts* was brought to *Christopher Southworth*, Priest ; shee answereth, that shee was brought to M. *Singletons* house by her owne Mother, where the said Priest was, and that shee further heard her said Mother say, after her Daughter had been in her fit, that shee should be brought vnto her Master, meaning the said Priest.

And shee further saith, that shee thinketh it was by and through the Counsell of the said M. *Thomson,* alias *Southworth*, Priest, That *Grace Sowerbuts* her Grandchild accused her of Witchcraft, and of such practises as shee is accused of : And thinketh further, the cause why the said *Thompson,* alias *Southworth* Priest, should practise with the Wench to doe it was, for that shee went to the Church.   *Iane*

Iane Southworth saith shee saw Master *Thompson*, alias *Southworth*, the Priest, a month or sixe weekes before she was committed to the Gaole ; and had conference with him in a place called Barne-hey-lane, where and when shee challenged him for slandering her to bee a Witch : wherunto he answered, that what he had heard thereof, he heard from her mother and her Aunt : yet she, this Examinate, thinketh in her heart it was by his procurement, and is moued so to thinke, for that shee would not be disswaded from the Church.

Ellen Bierley saith, Shee saw Master *Thompson*, alias *Southworth*, sixe or eight weeks before she was committed, and thinketh the said Priest was the practiser with *Grace Sowerbutts*, to accuse her of Witchcraft, and knoweth no cause why he should so doe, but because she goeth to the Church.

Signum, ✠ Iennet Bierley.

Signum, ⨎ Iane Southworth.

Signum, ⏀ Ellen Bierley.

William Leigh.

Edward Chisnall.

These

These Examinations being taken, they were brought into the Court, and there openly in the presence of this great Audience published, and declared to the Iurie of Life and Death; and thereupon the Gentlemen of their Iury required to consider of them. For although they stood vpon their Triall, for matter of Fact of Witchcraft, Murther, and much more of the like nature: yet in respect all their Accusations did appeare to bee practise: they were now to consider of them, and to acquit them. Thus were these poore Innocent creatures, by the great care and paines of this honorable Iudge, deliuered from the danger of this conspiracie; this bloudie practise of the Priest laid open: of whose fact I may lawfully say; *Etiam si ego tacuero clamabunt lapides.*

These are but ordinary with Priests and Iesuites: no respect of Bloud, kindred, or friendship, can moue them to forbeare their Conspiracies: for when he had laboured treacherously to seduce and conuert them, and yet could doe no good; then deuised he this meanes.

God of his great mercie deliuer vs all from them and their damnable conspiracies: and when any of his Maiesties subiects, so free and innocent as these, shall come in question, grant them as honorable a Triall, as Reuerend and worthy a Iudge to sit in Iudgement vpon them; and in the end as speedie a deliuerance. And for that which I haue heard of them; seene with my eyes, and taken paines to Reade of them: My humble prayer shall be to God Almightie. Vt Conuertantur ne pereant. Aut confundantur ne noceant.

To conclude, because the discourse of these three women of Salmesbury hath beene long and trouble-

some

some to you ; it is heere placed amongst the Witches, by special order and commandement, to set forth to the World the practise and conspiracie of this bloudy Butcher. And because I haue presented to your view a Kalender in the Frontispice of this Booke, of twentie notorious Witches : I shall shew you their deliuerance in order, as they came to their Arraignement and Triall euery day, and as the Gentlemen of euery Iury for life and death stood charged with them.

N3   THE

THE ARRAIGNMENT
and Triall of ANNE REDFERNE,
Daughter of ANNE WHITTLE, *alias* CHATTOX,
*of the Forrest of Pendle, in the Countie of Lancaster, for
Witchcraft ; vpon Wednesday the nineteenth of August,
at the Assises and Generall Gaole-deliuerie, holden at
Lancaster,*

Before
Sir EDVVARD BROMLEY *Knight, one of his Maiesties Iustices of Assise at Lancaster.*

Anne Redferne.

Vch is the horror of Murther, and the crying sinne of Bloud, that it will neuer bee
satisfied but with Bloud. So fell it out
with this miserable creature, *Anne Redferne*, the daughter of *Anne Whittle*, alias
Chattox : who, as shee was her Mother, and brought her
into the World, so was she the meanes to bring her into
this danger, and in the end to her Execution, for much
Bloud spilt, and many other mischiefes done.

For vpon Tuesday night (although you heare little
of her at the Arraignment and Triall of old *Chattox*,
her Mother) yet was shee arraigned for the murther of
Robert

Robert Nutter, and others : and by the fauour and mercifull consideration of the Iurie, the Euidence being not very pregnant against her, she was acquited, and found Not guiltie.

Such was her condition and course of life, as had she liued, she would haue beene very dangerous : for in making pictures of Clay, she was more cunning then any : But the innocent bloud yet vnsatisfied, and crying out vnto G O D for satisfaction and reuenge ; the crie of his people (to deliuer them from the danger of such horrible and bloudie executioners, and from her wicked and damnable practises) hath now againe brought her to a second Triall, where you shall heare what wee haue vpon Record against her.

This *Anne Redferne*, prisoner in the Castle at Lancaster, being brought to the Barre, before the great Seat of Iustice, was there, according to the former order and course, indicted and arraigned, for that she felloniously had practised, exercised, and vsed her deuillish and wicked Arts, called *Witchcrafts, Inchauntments, Charmes*, and *Sorceries*, in and vpon one *Christopher Nutter*, and him the said *Christopher Nutter*, by force of the same Witchcrafts, felloniously did kill and murther, *Contra formam Statuti &c. Et contra Pacem &c.*

Vpon her Arraignement to this Indictment, she pleaded *Not-Guiltie* ; and for the triall of her life put her selfe vpon G O D and the Countrey.

So as now the Gentlemen of the Iurie of Life and Death stand charged with her as with others.

The Euidence against Anne Redferne, *Prisoner at the Barre.*

The

The Examination of ELIZABETH

SOTHERNES, alias OLD DEMBDIKE, *taken at the Fence, in the Forrest of Pendle, in the Countie of Lancaster, the second day of Aprill*, Anno Reg. Regis IACOBI, Angliæ, &c. decimo, & Scotiæ xlv.

Against

ANNE REDFERNE (*the daughter of* ANNE WHITTLE, alias CHATTOX) *Prisoner at the Barre :*

Before

ROGER NOVVEL *of Reade, Esquire, one of his Maieslies Iuslices of Peace within the said Countie.*

THis Examinate saith, That about halfe a yeare before *Robert Nutter* died, as this Examinate thinketh, this Examinate went to the house of *Thomas Redferne*, which was about Midsummer, as shee this Examinate now remembreth it : and there, within three yards of the East end of the said house, shee saw the said *Anne Whittle* and *Anne Redferne*, wife of the said *Thomas Redferne*, and daughter of the said *Anne Whittle*, the one on the one side of a Ditch, and the other on the other side, and two pictures of Clay or Marle lying by them, and the third picture the said *Anne Whittle* was making. And the said *Anne Redferne*, her said daughter, wrought her Clay or Marle to make the third picture withall. And this Examinate passing by them, a Spirit, called *Tibbe*, in the shape of a blacke Cat, appeared vnto her this Examinate, and said, Turne backe againe, and doe as they doe. To whom this Examinate said, What are they doing ?

ing? Whereunto the said Spirit said, They are making three pictures: whereupon shee asked, whose pictures they were? whereunto the said Spirit said, They are the pictures of *Chriſtopher Nutter*, *Robert Nutter*, and *Mary*, wife of the said *Robert Nutter*. But this Examinate denying to goe backe to helpe them to make the pictures aforesaid, the said Spirit seeming to be angrie therefore, shot or pushed this Examinate into the Ditch; and so shedde the milke which this Examinate had in a Kanne, or Kitt: and so thereupon the Spirit at that time vanished out of this Examinates sight. But presently after that, the said Spirit appeared vnto this Examinate again in the shape of a Hare, and so went with her about a quarter of a myle, but said nothing vnto her this Examinate, nor shee to it.

The Examination *of* M A R G A R E T CROOKE

Againſt

the said A N N E R E D F E R N E: *Taken the day and yeare aforesaid,*

Before

R O G E R N O V V E L *aforesaid, Esquire, one of his Maieſties Iuſtices of the Peace in the Countie of Lancaſter.*

THis Examinate, sworne & examined vpon her oath, sayth, That about eighteene or nineteene yeares agoe, this Examinates brother, called *Robert Nutter*, about Whitsontide the same yeare, meeting with the said *Anne Redferne*, vpon some speeches betweene them they fell

out,

out, as this Examinats said brother told this Examinat :
and within some weeke, or fort-night, then next after,
this Examinats said brother fell sicke, and so languished
vntill about Candlemas then next after, and then died.
In which time of his sicknesse, he did a hundred times
at the least say, That the said *Anne Redferne* and her as-
sociates had bewitched him to death. And this Examinate further saith, That this Examinates Father, called
Chriſtopher Nutter, about Maudlintide next after following fell sicke, and so languished, vntill Michaelmas
then next after, and then died : during which time of his
sicknesse, hee did sundry times say, That hee was bewitched ; but named no bodie that should doe the same.

The Examination of I O H N N V T-
T E R, *of Higham Booth, in the Forreſt of Pendle, in the
Countie of Lancaſter, yeoman,*

Againſt
the said A N N E R E D F E R N E : *Taken the day and yeare
aforesaid,*

Before
R O G E R N O V V E L *Esquire, one of his Maieſties Iuſtices of Peace in the Countie of Lancaſter.*

THis Examinate, sworne & examined vpon his oath,
sayth, That in or about Chriſtmas, some eighteene
or nineteene years agoe, this Examinat comming from
Burnley with *Chriſtopher Nutter* and *Robert Nutter*, this
Examinates Father and Brother, this Examinate heard
                                                        his

his said Brother then say vnto his said Father these words, or to this effect. *Father, I am sure I am bewitched by the* Chattox, Anne Chattox, *and* Anne Redferne *her daughter, I pray you cause them to bee layed in Lancaster Castle :* Whereunto this Examinates Father answered, Thou art a foolish Ladde, it is not so, it is thy miscarriage. Then this Examinates Brother weeping, said ; nay, I am sure that I am bewitched by them, and if euer I come againe (for hee was readie to goe to Sir *Richard Shuttleworths,* then his Master) I will procure them to bee laid where they shall be glad to bite Lice in two with their teeth.

Hereupon *Anne Whittle,* alias *Chattox,* her Mother, was brought forth to bee examined, who confessed the making of the pictures of Clay, and in the end cried out very heartily to God to forgiue her sinnes, and vpon her knees intreated for this *Redferne,* her daughter.

Here was likewise many witnesses examined vpon oth *Viua`voce,* who charged her with many strange practises, and declared the death of the parties, all in such sort, and about the time in the Examinations formerly mentioned.

All men that knew her affirmed, shee was more dangerous then her Mother, for shee made all or most of the Pictures of Clay, that were made or found at any time.

Wherefore I leaue her to make good vse of the little time she hath to repent in : but no meanes could moue her to repentance, for as shee liued, so shee dyed.

The Examination of IAMES DEVICE,
taken the day and yeare afore-said.

Before
ROGER NOWEL, *and* NICHOLAS BANNE-
STER, *Esquires : two of his Maiesties Iustices of Peace
within the said Countie of Lancaster.* viz.

THe said Examinate vpon his oath saith, That about
two yeares agoe, hee this Examinate saw three Pictures of Clay, of halfe a yard long, at the end of *Redfernes* house, which *Redferne* had one of the Pictures in
his hand, *Marie* his Daughter had another in her hand,
Anne Redferne and the said *Redfernes* wife, now prisoner at Lancaster,
the Witch. had an other Picture in her hand, which Picture she the
said *Redfernes* wife, was then crumbling, but whose Pictures they were, this Examinate cannot tell. And at
his returning back againe, some ten Roods off them
there appeared vnto him this Examinate a
thing like a Hare, which spit fire
at him this Exami-
nate.

The

THE ARRAIGNMENT

and Triall of A L I C E N V T T E R,

*of the Forreſt of Pendle, in the Countie of Lancaſter, for
Witch-craft ; vpon Wedneſday the nineteenth of Auguſt,
at the Aſſizes and generall Gaole deliuerie, holden at Lancaſter.*

Before

Sir E D W A R D B R O M L E Y *Knight, one of his
Maieſties Iuſtices of Aſſize, at Lancaſter.*

Alice Nutter.

He two degrees of persons which chiefly
practiſe Witchcraft, are such, as are in
great miserie and pouertie, for such the
Deuill allures to follow him, by promiſing
great riches, and worldly commoditie ;
Others, though rich, yet burne in a desperate desire of
Reuenge ; Hee allures them by promises, to get their
turne satisfied to their hearts contentment, as in the
whole proceedings againſt old *Chattox :* the examinations of old *Dembdike* ; and her children, there was
not one of them, but haue declared the like, when the
Deuill first assaulted them.

But to attempt this woman in that sort, the Diuel had small meanes : For it is certaine she was a rich woman ; had a great estate, and children of good hope : in the common opinion of the world, of good temper, free from enuy or malice ; yet whether by the meanes of the rest of the Witches, or some vnfortunate occasion, shee was drawne to fall to this wicked course of life, I know not : but hither shee is now come to receiue her Triall, both for Murder, and many other vilde and damnable practises.

Great was the care and paines of his Lordship, to make triall of the Innocencie of this woman, as shall appeare vnto you vpon the Examination of *Iennet Deuice*, in open Court, at the time of her Arraignement and Triall ; by an extraordinary meanes of Triall, to marke her out from the rest.

It is very certaine she was of the Grand-counsell at Malking-Tower vpon Good-Friday, and was there present, which was a very great argument to condemne her.

This *Alice Nutter*, Prisoner in the Castle at Lancaster : Being brought to the Barre before the Great Seat of Iustice ; was there according to the former order and course Indicted and Arraigned, for that she felloniously had practised, exercised, and vsed her diuellish and wicked Arts, called *Witchcrafts, Inchantments, Charmes* and *Sorceries*, in and vpon *Henry Mitton* : and him the said *Henry Mitton*, by force of the same Witchcrafts, felloniously did kill and murther. *Contra formam Statuti*, &c. *Et Contra Pacem*, &c.

Vpon her Arraignement, to this Indictment shee pleaded not guiltie ; and for the triall of her life, put her ſelfe vpon God and the Countrey.

So as now the Gentlemen of the Iury of life and death ſtand charged with her, as with others.

The Euidence againſt Alice Nutter *Priſoner at the Barre.*

The Examination of IAMES DEVICE

ſonne of ELIZABETH DEVICE*: Taken the ſeuen and twentieth day of Aprill :* Anno Reg. Regis IACOBI Angliæ, Franciæ, & Hiberniæ, Fidei Defenſor. &c. Decimo & Scotiæ, xlvj.

Before

ROGER NOVVEL *and* NICHOLAS BANE-STER, *two of his* Maieſties Iuſtices of Peace in the Countie of Lancaſter. Againſt Alice Nutter.

THe ſaid Examinate ſaith vpon his oath, That hee heard his Grand-mother ſay, about a yeare ago, that his mother, called *Elizabeth Deuice,* and his Grand-mother, and the wife of *Richard Nutter,* of the Rough-Lee aforeſaid, had killed one *Henry Mitton,* of the Rough-Lee aforeſaid, by Witchcraft. The reaſon wherefore he was ſo killed, was for that this Examinats ſaid Grand-mother had asked the ſaid *Mitton* a penny : and hee denying her thereof ; thereupon ſhee procured his death as aforeſaid.

Alice Nutter the Priſoner

The

The Examination of ELIZABETH

DEVICE, *mother of the said* IAMES DEVICE.

Against

ALICE NVTTER, *wife of* RICHARD NVT-
TER, *Prisoner at the Barre, vpon her Arraignement and
Triall.*

Before

ROGER NOVVEL *and* NICHOLAS BANE-
TER, *Esquires, the day and yeare aforesaid.*

THis Examinate vpon her oath confesseth, and saith,
That she, with the wife of *Richard Nutter*, called *A-
lice Nutter*, Prisoner at the Barre ; and this Examinates
said mother, *Elizabeth Sotherne*, alias *Old Demdike* ; ioyned altogether, and bewitched the said *Henry Mitton* to
death.

This Examinate further saith, That vpon Good-friday last, there dined at this examinats house two women
of Burneley Parish, whose names the said *Richard Nutters* wife, *Alice Nutter*, now Prisoner at the Barre, doth
know.

The

The Examination of I A M E S D E-
V I C E *aforesaid,*

Against
The said A L I C E   N V T T E R, *the day and yeare a-foresaid.*

THe said Examinate vpon his oath saith, That vpon Good-Friday about twelue of the clocke in the day time, there dined in this Examinats said mothers house, a number of persons, whereof three were men, with this Examinate, and the rest women : and that they mette there for these three causes following, as this Examinats said mother told this Examinate.

The first was for the naming of the Spirit, which *Alizon Deuice*, now Prisoner at Lancaster, had, but did not name him, because she was not there.

The second cause was, for the deliuerie of his said Grand-mother ; this Examinates said sister, *Alizon* ; the said *Anne Chattox*, and her daughter *Redferne* ; killing the Gaoler at Lancaster, and before the next Assizes to blow vp the Castle there ; to the end that the foresaid Prisoners might by that meanes make an escape, and get away : all which this Examinate then heard them conferre of.

And he also saith, The names of such Witches as were on Good-Friday at this Examinats said Grand-mothers house, and now this Examinates owne mothers, for so many of them as he doth know, were amongst others, *Alice Nutter*, mother of *Myles Nutter*, now Prisoner at the Barre. And this Examinate further saith, That all the said Witches went out of the said house in their

P   owne

owne shapes and likenesses ; and they all, by that time
they were forth of the doores, were gotten on horse-
backe, like vnto Foales, some of one colour, and some of
another ; and *Preſtons* wife was the laſt : and when shee
got on horse-back, they all presently vanished out of this
Examinates sight : and before their said parting away,
they all appointed to meete at the said *Preſtons* wifes
house that day twelue month, at which time the said
Preſtons wife promised to make them a great feaſt : and
if they had occasion to meete in the meane time, then
should warning be giuen to meet vpō Romleys Moore.

The Examination and Euidence of IENNET DEVICE, *daughter of* ELIZABETH DEVICE.

Againſt
ALICE NVTTER, *Prisoner at the Barre.*

THe said Examinate saith, That on Good-Friday
laſt, there was about 20. persons, whereof only two
were men (to this Examinates remembrance) at her said
Grand-mothers house at Malking-Tower, about twelue
of the clock ; all which persons, this Examinats said mother tould her, were Witches. And she further saith, she
knoweth the names of six of them, *viz.* the wife of *Hugh
Hargreiues* vnder Pendle, *Chriſtopher Howgate* of Pendle,
Vncle to this Examinat and *Elizabeth* his wife ; and *Dick
Myles* wife of the Rough-Lee, *Chriſtopher Iacks* of Thor-
niholme, and his wife ; and the names of the residue, she
this Examinate doth not know.

AFter these Examinations were openly read, his
Lordship being very suspitious of the accusation of
this yong wench *Iennet Deuice*, commanded one to take
her away into the vpper Hall, intending in the meane
time to make Triall of her Euidence, and the Accusation especially against this woman, who is charged to haue
beene at Malking-Tower, at this great meeting. Master
Couel was commanded to set all his Prisoners by themselues, and betwixt euery Witch another Prisoner, and
some other strange women amongst them, so as no man
could iudge the one from the other : and these being set
in order before the Court from the prisoners, then was
the Wench *Iennet Deuice* commaunded to be brought
into the Court : and being set before my Lord, he tooke
great paines to examine her of euery particular Point,
What women were at Malking-Tower vpon Good-
Friday ? How she knew them ? What were the names of
any of them ? And how she knew them to be such as she
named ?

In the end being examined by my Lord, Whether
she knew them that were there by their faces, if she saw
them ? she told my Lord she should : whereupon in the
presence of this great Audience, in open Court, she went
and tooke *Alice Nutter*, this prisoner, by the hand, and
accused her to be one : and told her in what place shee
sat at the Feast at Malking-Tower, at the great assembly
of the Witches, and who sat next her : what conference
they had, and all the rest of their proceedings at large,
without any manner of contrarietie.

Being demaunded further by his Lordship, Whether
she knew *Iohan a Style* ? she alledged, she knew no such
womā to be there, neither did she euer heare her name.

This

This could be no forged or false Accusation, but the very Act of G o d to discouer her.

Thus was no meanes left to doe her all indifferent fauour, but it was vsed to saue her life ; and to this shee could giue no answere.

But nothing would serue: for old *Dembdike*, old *Chattox*, and others, had charged her with innocent bloud, which cries out for Reuenge, and will be satisfied. And therefore Almightie G o d, in his Iustice, hath cut her off.

And here I leaue her, vntill shee come to her Execution, where you shall heare shee died very impenitent ; insomuch as her owne children were neuer able to moue her to confesse any particular offence, or declare any thing, euen in *Articulo Mortis :* which was a very fearefull thing to all that were present, who knew shee was guiltie.

* *
*

THE

THE ARRAIGNMENT

and Triall of KATHERINE HEVVIT,
Wife of IOHN HEVVIT, *alias* MOVLD-HEELES,
*of Coulne, in the Countie of Lancaſter Clothier, for
Witchcraft ; vpon Wednesday the nineteenth of Auguſt,
at the Aſsises and Generall Gaole-deliuerie, holden at
Lancaſter.*

Before
Sir EDVVARD BROMLEY *Knight, one of his Maieſties Iuſtices of Aſsise at Lancaſter.*

Katherine Hewit.

Ho but Witches can be proofes, and so
witnesses of the doings of Witches? since
all their Meetings, Conspiracies, Practises,
and Murthers, are the workes of Darkenesse : But to discouer this wicked *Furie,*
GOD hath not onely raised meanes beyond expectation, by the voluntarie Confession and Accusation
of all that are gone before, to accuse this Witch (being Witches, and thereby witnesses of her doings)
but after they were committed, by meanes of a Child,
to discouer her to be one, and a Principall in that wicked assembly at Malking-Tower, to deuise such a damnable course for the deliuerance of their friends at

Lan-

Lancaſter, as to kill the Gaoler, and blow vp the Caſtle, wherein the Deuill did but labour to assemble them together, and so being knowne to send them all one way: And herein I shall commend vnto your good consideration the wonderfull meanes to condemne these parties, that liued in the world, free from suspicion of any such offences, as are proued againſt them: And thereby the more dangerous, that in the successe wee may lawfully say, the very Finger of God did point thē out. And she that neuer saw them, but in that meeting, did accuse them, and by their faces discouer them.

This *Katherine Hewyt*, Prisoner in the Caſtle at Lancaſter, being brought to the Barre before the great Seate of Iuſtice, was there according to the former order and course Indiĉted and Arraigned, for that she felloniously had practized, exercised, and vsed her Deuillish and wicked Arts, called *Witch-crafts, Inchantments, Charmes*, and *Sorceries*, in, and vpon *Anne Foulds*; and the same *Anne Foulds*, by force of the same witch-craft, felloniously did kill and murder. *Contra formam Statuti, &c. Et contra Pacem diĉti Domini Regū, &c.*

Vpon her Arraignement to this Indiĉtment, shee pleaded not guiltie; And for the triall of her life put her selfe vpon God and her Countrie.

So as now the Gentlemen of the Iurie of life and death, ſtand charged with her as with others.

The Euidence againſt Katherine Hewyt,
Prisoner at the Barre.

The

The Examination of IAMES DEVICE,

Sonne of ELIZABETH DEVICE, *taken the seuen and twentieth day of* April, Anno Reg. Regis IACOBI, Angliæ, Franciæ, & Hiberniæ, decimo, & Scotiæ quadragesimo quarto.

Before

ROGER NOWEL, *and* NICHOLAS BANNESTER, *Esquires ; two of his* Maiesties Iustices of Peace, *in the Countie of Lancaster.*

Against

KATHERINE HEWYT, *alias* MOVLD-HEELES *of Colne.* viz.

THis Examinate saith, that vpon Good-Friday last, about twelue of the Clock in the day time, there dined at this Examinates Mothers house a number of persons : And hee also saith, that they were Witches ; and that the names of the said Witches, that were there, for so many of them as he did know, were amongst others *Katherine Hewyt*, wife of *Iohn Hewyt*, alias *Mould-heeles*, of Colne, in the Countie of Lancaster Clothier ; And that the said Witch, called *Katherine Hewyt*, alias *Mouldheeles*, and one *Alice Gray*, did confesse amongst the said Witches at their meeting at *Malkin-Tower* aforesaid, that they had killed *Foulds* wifes child, called *Anne Foulds*, of Colne : And also said, that they had then in hanck a child of *Michael Hartleys* of Colne.

And this Examinate further saith, that all the said Witches went out of the said house in their own shapes and likenesses, and by that time they were gotten forth

of

of the doores, they were gotten on Horse-back like vnto foales, some of one colour, some of an other, and the
said *Preſtons* wife was the laſt : And when shee got on
Horse-back, they all presently vanished out of this Examinates sight. And before their said parting away they
all appointed to meete at the said *Preſtons* wifes house
that day twelue Moneths : at which time the said *Preſtons* wife promised to make them a great feaſt, and if
they had occasion to meete in the meane time, then
should warning be giuen that they all should meet vpon
Romlesmoore.

The Examination and Euidence of
ELIZABETH DEVICE, *Mother of the said* IAMES
DEVICE,

Againſt
KATHERINE HEWYT, *alias* MOVLD-HEELES,
*Prisoner at the Barre vpon her Arraignement and Triall,
taken the day and yeare aforesaid.* viz.

THis Examinate vpon her oath confesseth, that vpon
Good-Friday laſt there dyned at this Examinates
house, which she hath said are Witches, and verily thinketh to bee Witches, such as the said *Iames Deuice* hath
formerly spoken of ; amongſt which was *Katherine Hewyt*, alias *Mould-heeles*, now Prisoner at the Barre : and
shee also saith, that at their meeting on Good-Friday at
Malkin-Tower aforesaid, the said *Katherine Hewyt*, alias
Mould-heeles, and *Alice Gray*, did confesse, they had killed

led a child of *Foulds* of Colne, called *Anne Foulds*, and had gotten hold of an other.

And shee further saith, the said *Katherine Hewyt* with all the reſt, there gaue her consent with the said *Preſtons* wife for the murder of Maſter *Liſter*.

The Examination and Euidence of IENNET DEVICE,

Against KATHERINE HEWYT, *alias* MOVLD-HEELES, *Prisoner at the Barre.*

THe said Examinate saith, That vpon Good-Friday laſt, there was about twentie persons, where of two were men to this Examinates remembrance, at her said Grand-mothers house, called *Malkin-Tower* aforesaid, about twelue of the clock : All which persons this Examinates said mother told her were Witches, and that shee knoweth the names of sixe of the said Witches.

Then was the said *Iennet Deuice* commanded by his Lordship, to finde and point out the said *Katherine Hewyt*, alias *Mould-heeles*, amongſt all the reſt of the said Women, whereupon shee went and tooke the said *Katherine Hewyt* by the hand: Accused her to bee one, and told her in what place shee sate at the feaſt at *Malkin-Tower*, at the great Assembly of the Witches, and who sate next her ; what conference they had, and all the reſt of their proceedings at large, without any manner of contrarietie : Being demanded further by his Lord-

Q   ship,

ship, whether *Ioane a Downe* were at that Feast, and meeting, or no? shee alleaged shee knew no such woman to
be there, neither did shee euer heare her name.

If this were not an Honorable meanes to trie the accusation against them, let all the World vpon due examination giue iudgement of it. And here I leaue her
the last of this companie, to the Verdict of the Gentlemen of the Iurie of life and death, as hereafter shall appeare.

Heere the Iurie of Life and Death, hauing spent the
most part of the day, in due consideration of their offences; Returned into the Court to deliuer vp their Verdict against them, as followeth.

The Verdict of Life and Death.

WHo vpon their Oathes found *Iennet Bierley*, *Ellen
Bierley*, and *Iane Southworth*, not guiltie of the
offence of Witch-craft, conteyned in the Indictment a-
gainst them.

Anne Redferne, guiltie of the fellonie & murder, conteyned in the Indictment against her.

Alice Nutter, guiltie of the fellonie and murder conteyned in the Indictment against her.

And
Katherine Hewyt, guiltie of the fellonie & murder conteyned in the Indictment against her.

Where-

Whereupon Master *Couell* was commanded by the Court to take away the Prisoners Conuicted, and to bring forth *Iohn Bulcocke*, *Iane Bulcocke* his mother, and *Alizon Deuice*, Prisoners in the Castle at Lancaster, to receiue their Trialls.

Who were brought to their Arraigne ent and Triall as hereafter followeth.

Q 2   THE

THE ARRAIGNMENT

and Triall of I O H N B V L C O C K,
and I A N E B V L C O C K *his mother, wife of* CHRI-
STOPHER BVLCOCK, *of the Mosse-end, in the Countie of Lancaster, for Witch-craft : vpon Wednesday in the
after-noone, the nineteenth of August, 1612. At the Assizes and generall Gaole deliuery, holden at Lancaster.*

Before
Sir EDVVARD BROMLEY, *Knight, one of his Maiesties Iustices of Assizes at Lancaster.*

John Bulcock,
and
Jane Bulcock his mother.

I F there were nothing to charge these Prisoners withall, whom now you may behold vpon their Arraignment and Triall but their poasting in haste to the great
Assembly at Malking-Tower, there to
aduise and consult amongst the Witches, what were to
bee done to set at liberty the Witches in the Castle at
Lancaster : Ioyne with *Iennet Preston* for the murder of
Master *Lister* ; and such like wicked & diuellish practises:

It

It were sufficient to accuse them for Witches, & to bring their liues to a lawfull Triall. But amongst all the Witches in this company, there is not a more fearefull and diuellish Act committed, and voluntarily confessed by any of them, comparable to this, vnder the degree of Murder: which impudently now (at the Barre hauing formerly confessed;) they forsweare, swearing they were neuer at the great assembly at Malking Tower; although the very Witches that were present in that action with them, iustifie, maintaine, and sweare the same to be true against them: Crying out in very violent & outragious manner, euen to the gallowes, where they died impenitent for any thing we know, because they died silent in the particulars. These of all others were the most desperate wretches (void of all feare or grace) in all this Packe; Their offences not much inferiour to Murther: for which you shall heare what matter of Record wee haue against them; and whether they be worthie to continue, we leaue it to the good consideration of the Iury.

The said *Iohn Bulcock*, and *Iane Bulcock* his mother, Prisoners in the Castle at Lancaster, being brought to the Barre before the great Seat of Iustice: were there according to the former order and course Indicted and Arraigned, for that they felloniously had practised, exercised and vsed their diuellish & wicked Arts, called *Witchcrafts, Inchantments, Charmes* and *Sorceries*, in and vpon the body of *Iennet Deane*: so as the body of the said *Iennet Deane*, by force of the said Witchcrafts, wasted and consumed; and after she, the said *Iennet*, became madde. *Contra formam Statuti*, &c. *Et Contra Pacem*, &c.

Vpon their Arraignement, to this Indictment they pleaded not guiltie; and for the triall of their liues put

them-

themselues vpon God and their Countrey.

So as now the Gentlemen of the Iurie of Life and Death stand charged with them as with others.

The Euidence against Iohn Bulcock, *and* Iane Bulcock *his mother, Prisoners at the Barre.*

The Examination of IAMES DEVICE
taken the seuen and twentieth day of Aprill aforesaid.

Before
ROGER NOVVEL *and* NICHOLAS BANE-STER, *Esquires, two of his Maiesties Iustices of Peace in the Countie of Lancaster.*

Against
IOHN BVLCOCK *and* IANE BVLCOCK *his mother.*

THis Examinate saith, That vpon Good-Friday, about twelue of the clocke in the day time, there dined in this Examinates said Mothers house a number of persons, whereof three were men with this Examinate, and the rest women, and that they met there for these three causes following, as this Examinates said mother told this Examinate. The first was, for the naming of the Spirit which *Allison Deuice*, now prisoner at Lancaster had, but did not name him, because shee was not there. The second cause was, for the deliuerie of his said Grand-mother; this Examinates said sister *Allison*; the said *Anne Chattox*, and her daughter *Redferne*, killing
the

the Gaoler at Lancaster, and before the next Assises to blow vp the Castle there, to that end the aforesaid prisoners might by that meanes make an escape, and get away : All which this Examinate then heard them conferre of.

And he also sayth, That the names of such said Witches as were on Good-Friday at this Examinates said Grand-mothers house, and now this Examinates owne mothers, for so many of them as hee did know, were these, *viz. Iane Bulcock*, wife of *Christopher Bulcock*, of the Mosse end, and *Iohn* her sonne amongst others, &c.

And this Examinate further saith, That all the said Witches went out of the said house in their own shapes and likenesses : and they all, by that they were forth of the dores, were gotten on horse-backe, like vnto Foales, some of one colour, and some of another, and *Prestons* wife was the last : and when shee got on horse-backe, they all presently vanished out of this Examinates sight.

And further he saith, That the said *Iohn Bulcock* and *Iane* his said Mother, did confesse vpon Good-Friday last, at the said Malking-Tower, in the hearing of this Examinate, That they had bewitched, at the new-field Edge in Yorkshire, a woman called *Iennet*, wife of *Iohn Deyne*, besides, her Reason ; and the said Womans name so bewitched, he did not heare them speake of And this Examinate further saith, That at the said Feast at Malking-Tower this Examinate heard them all giue their consents to put the said Master *Thomas Lister* of Westby to death. And after Master *Lister* should be made away by Witch-craft, then all the said Witches gaue their consents to ioyne all together, to hanck Ma-

ster

ster *Leonard Lister*, when he should come to dwell at the Cow-gill, and so put him to death.

The Examination of ELIZABETH DEVICE, *Taken the day and yeare aforesaid,*

Before

ROGER NOVVEL *and* NICHOLAS BANE-STER, *Esquires, two of his Maiesties Iustices of Peace in the Countie of Lancaster,*

Against

IOHN BVLCOCK, *and* IANE BVLCOCK, *his mother.*

THis Examinate saith vpon her oath, That she doth verily thinke, that the said *Bulcockes* wife doth know of some Witches to bee about Padyham and Burnley.

And shee further saith, That at the said meeting at Malking-Tower, as aforesaid, *Katherine Hewit* and *Iohn Bulcock*, with all the rest then there, gaue their consents, with the said *Prestons* wife, for the killing of the said Master *Lister*.

The

The Examination and Euidence of
IENNET DEVICE
Againſt
IOHN BVLCOCKE *and* IANE *his mother, prisoners at the Barre.*

THe said Examinate saith, That vpon Good-Friday laſt there was about twentie persons, whereof two were men, to this Examinates remembrance, at her said Grand-mothers house, called Malking-Tower aforesaid : all which persons, this Examinates said mother told her were Witches, and that she knoweth the names of sixe of the said Witches.

Then was the said *Iennet Deuice* commaunded by his Lordship to finde and point out the said *Iohn Bulcock* and *Iane Bulcock* amongſt all the reſt : whereupon shee went and tooke *Iane Bulcock* by the hand, accused her to be one, and told her in what place shee sat at the Feaſt at Malking-Tower, at the great Assembly of the Witches ; and who sat next her : and accused the said *Iohn Bulcock* to turne the Spitt there ; what conference they had, and all the reſt of their proceedings at large, without any manner of contrarietie.

Shee further told his Lordship, there was a woman that came out of Craven to that Great Feaſt at Malking-Tower, but shee could not finde her out amongſt all those women.

The

¶ The names of the Witches at the
Great Assembly and Feast at
Malking-Tower, *viz.* vpon Good-
Friday laſt, 1 6 1 2.

Elizabeth Deuice.

Alice Nutter.

Katherine Hewit, alias
Mould-heeles.

John Bulcock.

Jane Bulcock.

Alice Graie.

Jennet Hargraues.

Elizabeth Hargraues.

Christopher Howgate,
Sonne to old *Dembdike.*

Christopher Hargraues.
     Grace

Grace Hay, of Padiham.

Anne Crunckſhey, of Marchden.

Elizabeth Howgate.

Jennet Preſton, Executed at Yorke for the Murder of Maſter *Liſter.*

With many more, which being bound ouer to appeare at the laſt Assizes, are since that time fled to saue themselues.

The

THE ARRAIGNMENT
and Triall of ALIZON DEVICE,
Daughter of ELIZABETH DEVICE, *within the Forrest of Pendle, in the Countie of Lancaster aforesaid, for Witch-craft.*

Alizon Deuice.

BEhold, aboue all the rest, this lamentable spectacle of a poore distressed Pedler; how miserably hee was tormented, and what punishment hee endured for a small offence, by the wicked and damnable practise of this odious Witch, first instructed therein by old *Dembdike* her Grand-mother, of whose life and death with her good conditions, I haue written at large before in the beginning of this worke, out of her owne Examinations and other Records, now remayning with the Clarke of the Crowne at Lancaster : And by her Mother brought vp in this detestable course of life ; wherein I pray you obserue but the manner and course of it in order, euen to the last period at the Execution, for this horrible fact, able to terrifie and astonish any man liuing.

This *Alizon Deuice*, Prisoner in the Castle of Lancaster,

ster, being brought to the Barre before the great Seat of Iustice, was there according to the former order and course indicted and arraigned, for that shee felloniously had practised, exercised, and vsed her Deuillish and wicked Arts, called *Witch-craftes*, *Inchantments*, *Charmes*, and *Sorceries*, in, and vpon one *Iohn Law*, a Petti-chapman, and him had lamed, so that his bodie wasted and consumed, &c. *Contra formam Statuti, &c. Et contra pacem dicti Domini Regis, Coronam & Dignitatem, &c.*

Vpon the Arraignement, The poore Pedler, by name *Iohn Law*, being in the Castle about the Moot-hall, attending to be called, not well able to goe or stand, being led thether by his poore sonne *Abraham Law*: My Lord *Gerrard* moued the Court to call the poore Pedler, who was there readie, and had attended all the Assizes, to giue euidence for the Kings Majestie, against the said *Alizon Deuice*, Prisoner at the Barre, euen now vpon her Triall. The Prisoner being at the Barre, & now beholding the Pedler, deformed by her Witch-craft, and transformed beyond the course of Nature, appeared to giue euidence against her ; hauing not yet pleaded to her Indictment, saw it was in vaine to denie it, or stand vpon her justification : Shee humbly vpon her knees at the Barre with weeping teares, prayed the Court to heare her.

Whereupon my Lord *Bromley* commanded shee should bee brought out from the Prisoners neare vnto the Court, and there on her knees, shee humbly asked forgiuenesse for her offence : And being required to make an open declaration or confession of her offence : Shee confessed as followeth. *viz.*

The

The Confession of A L I Z O N D E-

V I C E, *Prisoner at the Barre : published and declared
at time of her Arraignement and Triall in open Court.*

SHe saith, That about two yeares agone, her Grand-
mother, called *Elizabeth Sothernes*, alias *Dembdike*, did
(sundry times in going or walking together, as they
went begging) perswade and aduise this Examinate to
let a Diuell or a Familiar appeare to her, and that shee,
this Examinate would let him suck at some part of her ;
and she might haue and doe what shee would. And so
not long after these perswasions, this Examinate being
walking towards the Rough-Lee, in a Close of one *Iohn
Robinsons*, there appeared vnto her a thing like vnto a
Blacke Dogge : speaking vnto her, this Examinate, and
desiring her to giue him her Soule, and he would giue
her power to doe any thing she would : whereupon this
Examinate being therewithall inticed, and setting her
downe ; the said Blacke-Dogge did with his mouth (as
this Examinate then thought) sucke at her breast, a little
below her Paps, which place did remaine blew halfe a
yeare next after : which said Blacke-Dogge did not appeare to this Examinate, vntill the eighteenth day of
March last : at which time this Examinate met with a
Pedler on the high-way, called Colne-field, neere vnto
Colne : and this Examinate demanded of the said Pedler to buy some pinnes of him ; but the said Pedler stur-
dily answered this Examinate that he would not loose
his Packe ; and so this Examinate parting with him : presently there appeared to this Examinate the Blacke-
Dogge, which appeared vnto her as before : which Black

Dogge

Dogge spake vnto this Examinate in English, saying ;
What wouldst thou haue me to do vnto yonder man ? to
whom this Examinate said, What canst thou do at him?
and the Dogge answered againe, I can lame him : whereupon this Examinat answered, and said to the said Black
Dogge, Lame him : and before the Pedler was gone fortie Roddes further, he fell downe Lame : and this Examinate then went after the said Pedler ; and in a house
about the distance aforesaid, he was lying Lame : and so
this Examinate went begging in Trawden Forrest that
day, and came home at night : and about fiue daies next
after, the said Black-Dogge did appeare to this Examinate, as she was going a begging, in a Cloase neere the
New-Church in Pendle, and spake againe to her, saying ;
Stay and speake with me ; but this Examinate would
not : Sithence which time this Examinat neuer saw him.

> *Which agreeth* verbatim *with her owne Exami-*
> *nation taken at* Reade, *in the Countie of*
> *Lancaster, the thirtieth day of* March, *be-*
> *fore Master* Nowel, *when she was apprehen-*
> *ded and taken.*

MY Lord *Bromley*, and all the whole Court not a
little wondering, as they had good cause, at this
liberall and voluntarie confession of the Witch ; which
is not ordinary with people of their condition and quali-
tie : and beholding also the poore distressed Pedler, standing by, commanded him vpon his oath to declare the
manner how, and in what sort he was handled ; how he
came to be lame, and so to be deformed ; who deposed
vpon his oath, as followeth.

The

The Euidence of I O H N L A VV,

Pettie Chapman, vpon his oath :

Againſt
A L I Z O N D E V I C E, *Prisoner at the Barre.*

HE deposeth and saith, That about the eighteenth of
March laſt paſt, hee being a Pedler, went with his
Packe of wares at his backe thorow Colne-field : where
vnluckily he met with *Alizon Deuice*, now Prisoner at
the Barre, who was very earneſt with him for pinnes, but
he would giue her none : whereupon she seemed to be
very angry ; and when hee was paſt her, hee fell downe
lame in great extremitie ; and afterwards by meanes got
into an Ale-house in Colne, neere vnto the place where
hee was firſt bewitched : and as hee lay there in great
paine, not able to ſtirre either hand or foote ; he saw a
great Black-Dogge ſtand by him, with very fearefull fi-
rie eyes, great teeth, and a terrible countenance, looking
him in the face ; whereat he was very sore afraid : and
immediately after came in the said *Alizon Deuice*, who
ſtaid not long there, but looked on him, and went away.

After which time hee was tormented both day and
night with the said *Alizon Deuice* ; and so continued
lame, not able to trauell or take paines euer since that
time : which with weeping teares in great passion turned to the Prisoner ; in the hearing of all the Court hee
said to her, *This thou knoweſt to be too true* : and thereupon she humblie acknowledged the same, and cried out
to God to forgiue her ; and vpon her knees with weeping teares, humbly prayed him to forgiue her that wicked offence ; which he very freely and voluntarily did.

Here

Hereupon Master *Nowel* standing vp, humbly prayed the fauour of the Court, in respect this Fact of Witchcraft was more eminent and apparant then the rest, that for the better satisfaction of the Audience, the Examination of *Abraham Law* might be read in Court.

The Examination of ABRAHAM

LAVV, *of Hallifax, in the Countie of Yorke, Cloth-dier,*
taken vpon oath the thirtieth day of March, 1612.

Before
ROGER NOVVEL, *Esquire, aforesaid.*

BEing sworne and examined, saith, That vpon Saturday last saue one, being the one and twentieth day of this instant March, he, this Examinate was sent for, by a letter that came from his father, that he should come to his father, *Iohn Law,* who then lay in Colne speechlesse, and had the left-side lamed all saue his eye : and when this Examinate came to his father, his said father had something recouered his speech, and did complaine that hee was pricked with Knives, Elsons and Sickles, and that the same hurt was done vnto him at Colne-field, presently after that *Alizon Deuice* had offered to buy some pinnes of him, and she had no money to pay for them withall ; but as this Examinates father told this Examinate, he gaue her some pinnes. And this Examinate further saith, That he heard his said father say that the hurt he had in his lamenesse was done vnto him by the said *Alizon Deuice,* by Witchcraft. And this

S   Exami-

Examinate further saith, that hee heard his said Father further say, that the said *Alizon Deuice* did lie vpon him and trouble him. And this Examinate seeing his said Father so tormented with the said *Alizon* and with one other olde woman, whome this Examinates Father did not know as it seemed : This Examinate made search after the said *Alizon*, and hauing found her, brought her to his said Father yesterday being the nine & twentieth of this instant March : whose said Father in the hearing of this Examinate and diuers others did charge the said *Alizon* to haue bewitched him, which the said *Alizon* confessing did aske this Examinates said Father forgiuenesse vpon her knees for the same ; whereupon this Examinates Father accordingly did forgiue her. Which Examination in open Court vpon his oath hee iustified to be true.

Whereupon it was there affirmed to the Court that this *Iohn Law* the Pedler, before his vnfortunate meeting with this Witch, was a verie able sufficient stout man of Bodie, and a goodly man of Stature. But by this Deuilish art of *Witch-craft* his head is drawne awrie, his Eyes and face deformed, His speech not well to bee vnderstood ; his Thighes and Legges starcke lame : his Armes lame especially the left side, his handes lame and turned out of their course, his Bodie able to indure no trauell : and thus remaineth at this present time.

The Prisoner being examined by the Court whether shee could helpe the poore Pedler to his former strength and health, she answer. she could not, and so did many of the rest of the Witches : But shee, with others, affirmed, That if old *Dembdike* had liued, shee could and would haue helped him out of that great miserie

serie, which so long he hath endured for so small an offence, as you haue heard.

These things being thus openly published againſt her,
and she knowing her selfe to be guiltie of euery particular, humbly acknowledged the Indictment againſt her
to be true, and that she was guiltie of the offence therein contained, and that she had iuſtly deserued death for
that and many other such like : whereupon she was carried away, vntill she should come to the Barre to receiue
her judgement of death.

Oh, who was present at this lamentable spectacle,
that was not moued with pitie to behold it *!*

Hereupon my Lord *Gerard*, Sir *Richard Houghton*, and
others, who much pitied the poore Pedler, At the en-
treatie of my Lord *Bromley* the Iudge, promised some
present course should be taken for his reliefe and maintenance ; being now discharged and sent away.

But here I may not let her passe ; for that I find some
thing more vpon Record to charge her withall : for although she were but a young Witch, of a yeares ſtanding, and thereunto induced by *Dembdike* her Grand-
mother, as you haue formerly heard, yet she was spotted with innocent bloud among the reſt : for in one part
of the Examination of *Iames Deuice*, her brother, he deposeth as followeth, *viz.*

The

The Examination of IAMES DE-VICE, *brother to the said* ALIZON DEVICE: *Taken vpon Oath*

Before

ROGER NOVVEL *Esquire, aforesaid, the thirtieth day of March,* 1612.

IAmes *Deuice*, of the Forrest of Pendle, in the Countie of Lancaster, Labourer, sworne and examined, sayth, That about Saint *Peters* day last one *Henry Bulcock* came to the house of *Elizabeth Sothernes*, alias *Dembdike*, Grand-mother to this Examinate, and said, That the said *Alizon Deuice* had bewitched a Child of his, and desired her, that shee would goe with him to his house : which accordingly shee did : and thereupon shee the said *Alizon* fell downe on her knees, and asked the said *Bulcock* forgiuenesse; and confessed to him, that she had bewitched the said Child, as this Examinate heard his said sister confesse vnto him this Examinate.

And although shee were neuer indicted for this offence, yet being matter vpon Record, I thought it conuenient to joyne it vnto her former Fact.

HEre the Iurie of Life and Death hauing spent the most part of the day in due consideration of their offences, returned into the Court to deliuer vp their Verdict against them, as followeth.

The

The Verdict of Life and Death.

WHo vpon their Oathes found *Iohn Bulcock* and *Iane Bulcock* his mother not guiltie of the Felonie by Witch-craft, contained in the Indictment against them.

Alizon Deuice conuicted vpon her owne Confession.

Whereupon Master *Couel* was commaunded by the Court to take away the Prisoners conuicted, and to bring forth *Margaret Pearson*, and *Isabell Robey*, Prisoners in the Castle at Lancaster, to receiue their Triall.

Who were brought to their Arraignement and Trialls, as hereafter followeth, *viz*.

S 3   THE

THE ARRAIGNMENT

and Triall of MARGARET PEAR-
SON *of Paddiham, in the Countie of Lancaster, for
Witchcraft; the nineteenth of August* 1612. *at the
Assises and Generall Gaole-deliuerie, holden at Lan-
caster,*

Before
Sir EDVVARD BROMLEY *Knight, one of his Maiesties Iustices of Assise at Lancaster.*

Margaret Pearson.

THus farre haue I proceeded in hope your
patience will endure the end of this discourse, which craues time, and were better not begunne at all, then not perfected.
This *Margaret Pearson* was the wife of
Edward Pearson of Paddiham, in the Countie of Lancaster; little inferiour in her wicked and malicious course
of life to any that hath gone before her : A very dangerous Witch of long continuance, generally suspected
and feared in all parts of the Countrie, and of all good
people neare her, and not without great cause: For who-
soeuer gaue her any iust occasion of offence, shee tormented

mented with great miserie, or cut off their children, goods, or friends.

This wicked and vngodly Witch reuenged her furie vpon goods, so that euery one neare her sustained great losse. I place her in the end of these notorious Witches, by reason her iudgement is of an other Nature, according to her offence ; yet had not the fauour and mercie of the Iurie beene more then her desert, you had found her next to old *Dembdike* ; for this is the third time shee is come to receiue her Triall ; one time for murder by Witch-craft ; an other time for bewitching a Neighbour ; now for goods.

> How long shee hath beene a Witch, the Deuill
> and shee knowes best.

The Accusations, Depositions, and particular Examinations vpon Record against her are infinite, and were able to fill a large Volume ; But since shee is now only to receiue her Triall for this last offence. I shall proceede against her in order, and set forth what matter we haue vpon Record, to charge her withall.

This *Margaret Pearson*, Prisoner in the Castle at Lancaster : Being brought to the Barre before the great Seat of Iustice ; was there according to the course and order of the Law Indicted and Arraigned, for that shee had practised, exercised, and vsed her diuellish and wicked Arts, called *Witchcrafts*, *Iuchantments*, *Charmes* and *Sorceries*, and one Horse or Mare of the goods and Chattels of one *Dodgeson* of Padiham, in the Countie of Lancaster, wickedly, maliciously, and voluntarily did kill. *Contra formam Statuti, &c. Et contra Pacem dicti Domini Regu. &c.*

Vpon

Vpon her Arraignement to this Indictment, shee pleaded not guiltie ; And for the triall of her life put her selfe vpon God and her Countrie.

So as now the Gentlemen of the Iurie of her offence and death, stand charged with her as with others.

The Euidence against Margaret Pearson,
Prisoner at the Barre.

The Examination and Euidence of Anne Whittle, *alias* Chattox.

Against
Margaret Pearson, *Prisoner at the Barre.*

THe said *Anne Chattox* being examined saith, That the wife of one *Pearson* of Paddiham, is a very euill Woman, and confessed to this Examinate, that shee is a Witch, and hath a Spirit which came to her the first time in likenesse of a Man, and clouen footed, and that shee the said *Pearsons* wife hath done very much harme to one *Dodgesons* goods, who came in at a loope-hole into the said *Dodgesons* Stable, and shee and her Spirit together did sit vpon his Horse or Mare, vntill the said Horse or Mare died. And likewise, that shee the said *Pearsons* wife did confesse vnto her this Examinate, that shee bewitched vnto death one *Childers* wife, and her Daughter, and that shee the said *Pearsons* wife is as ill as shee.

The

The Examination of IENNET BOOTH,

of Paddiham, in the Countie of Lancaſter, the ninth day of Auguſt 1612.

Before

NICHOLAS BANNESTER, *Esquire ; one of hĩ Maieſties Iuſtices of Peace in the Countie of Lancaſter.*

IEnnet, the wife of *Iames Booth*, of Paddiham, vpon her oath saith, That the Friday next after, the said *Pearsons* wife, was committed to the Gaole at Lancaſter, this Examinate was carding in the said *Pearsons* house, hauing a little child with her, and willed the said *Margerie* to giue her a little Milke, to make her said child a little meat, who fetcht this Examinate some, and put it in a pan ; this examinat meaning to set it on the fire, found the said fire very ill, and taking vp a ſtick that lay by her, and brake it in three or foure peeces, and laid vpon the coales to kindle the same, then set the pan and milke on the fire : and when the milke was boild to this Examinates content, she tooke the pan wherein the milke was, off the said fire, and with all, vnder the bottome of the same, there came a Toade, or a thing very like a Toade, and to this Examinates thinking came out of the fire, together with the said Pan, and vnder the bottome of the same, and that the said *Margerie* did carrie the said Toade out of the said house in a paire of tonges ; But what shee the said *Margerie* did therewith, this Examinate ĸ oweth not.

After this were diuers witnesses examined againſt her in open Court, *viua voce*, to proue the death of the Mare,

T   and

and diuers other vild and odious practises by her committed, who vpon their Examinations made it so apparant to the Iurie as there was no question ; But because
the fact is of no great importance, in respect her life is
not in question by this Indictment, and the Depositions
and examinations are many, I leaue to trouble you with
any more of them, for being found guiltie of this offence, the penaltie of the Law is as much as her good
Neighbours doe require, which is to be deliuered from the companie of such a
dangerous, wicked, and malicious Witch.

* *
*

The

THE ARRAIGNMENT

and Triall of ISABEL ROBEY

in the Countie of Lancaster, for Witch-craft : vpon Wednesday the nineteenth of August, 1612. At the Assizes and generall Gaole-deliuery, holden at Lancaster.

Before
Sir EDVVARD BROMLEY, *Knight, one of his Maiesties Iustices of Assizes at Lancaster.*

Isabel Robey.

THus at one time may you behold Witches of all sorts from many places in this Countie of Lancaster which now may lawfully bee said to abound asmuch in Witches of diuers kindes as Seminaries, Iesuites, and Papists. Here then is the last that came to act her part in this lamentable and wofull Tragedie, wherein his Maiestie hath lost so many Subjects, Mothers their Children, Fathers their Friends, and Kinsfolkes the like whereof hath not beene set forth in any age. What hath the Kings Maiestie written and published in his *Dæmonologie*, by way of premonition and preuention, which hath not here by the first or last

T 2 beene

beene executed, put in practise or discouered? What Witches haue euer vpon their Arraignement and Trial made s ᴄh open liberall and voluntarie declarations of their liues, and such confessions of their offences: The manner of their attempts and their bloudie practises, their meetings, consultations and what not? Therefore I shall now conclude with this *Isabel Robey* who is now come to her triall.

This *Isabel Robey* Prisoner in the Castle at Lancaster being brought to the Barre before the great Seat of Iustice was there according to the former order and course Indicted and Arraigned, for that shee Felloniously had practised, exercised and vsed her Deuilish and wicked Artes called *Witchcrafts, Inchantmnnts, Charmes and Sorceries.*

Vpon her Arraignment to this Indictment she pleaded not guiltie, and for the triall of her life, put her selfe vpon God and her Countrie.

So as now the Gentlemen of the Iurie of life and death stand charged with her as with others.

The Euidence against Isabel Robey
Prisoner at the Barre.

The

The Examination of PETER CHAD-

DOCK *of Windle, in the Countie of Lancaster: Taken at Windle aforesaid, the* 12. *day of Iuly* 1612. Anno Reg. Regis IACOBI, Angliæ, &c. decimo, & Scotiæ xlv.

Before

Sir THOMAS GERRARD *Knight, and Barronet. One of his Maiesties Iustices of the Peace within the said Countie.*

THe said Examinate vpon his Oath saith, That before his Marriage hee heard say that the said *Isabel Robey* was not pleased that hee should marrie his now wife: whereupon this Examinate called the said *Isabel* Witch, and said that hee did not care for her. Then within two dayes next after this Examinate was sore pained in his bones: And this Examinate hauing occasion to meete Master *Iohn Hawarden* at Peaseley Crosse, wished one *Thomas Lyon* to goe thither with him, which they both did so; but as they came home-wards, they both were in euill case. But within a short time after, this Examinate and the said *Thomas Lyon* were both very well amended.

And this Examinate further saith, that about foure yeares last past, his now wife was angrie with the said *Isabel*, shee then being in his house, and his said Wife thereupon went out of the house, and presently after that the said *Isabel* went likewise out of the house not well pleased, as this Examinate then did thinke, and presently after vpon the same day, this Examinate with his said wife working in the Hay, a paine and a starknesse fell into the necke of this Examinat which grieued him very

T 3   sore;

sore; wherupo this Examinat sent to one *Iames* a Glouer, which then dwelt in Windle, and desired him to pray for him, and within foure or fiue dayes next after this Examinate did mend very well. Neuerthelesse this Examinate during the same time was very sore pained, and so thirstie withall, and hot within his body, that hee would haue giuen any thing hee had, to haue slaked his thirst, hauing drinke enough in the house, and yet could not drinke vntill the time that the said *Iames* the Glouer came to him, and this Examinate then said before the said Glouer, I would to God that I could drinke, where upon the said Glouer said to this Examinate, take that drinke, and in the name of the *Father*, the *Sonne*, and the *Holy Ghost*, drinke it, saying; The Deuill and Witches are not able to preuaile against G O D and his Word, whereupon this Examinate then tooke the glasse of drinke, and did drinke it all, and afterwards mended very well, and so did continue in good health, vntill our Ladie day in Lent was twelue moneth or thereabouts, since which time this Examinate saith, that hee hath beene sore pained with great warch in his bones, and all his limmes, and so yet continueth, and this Examinate further saith, that his said warch and paine came to him rather by meanes of the said *Isabel Robey*, then otherwise, as he verily thinketh.

The

The Examination of I A N E W I L K I N-SON, *Wife of* FRANCIS WILKINSON, *of Windle a-foreſaid: Taken before the ſaid Sir* THOMAS GER-RARD, *Knight and Barronet, the day and place aforeſaid. Againſt the ſaid* ISABEL ROBEY.

THe said Examinate vpon her oath saith, that vpon a time the said *Isabel Robey* asked her milke, and shee denied to giue her any: And afterwards shee met the said *Isabel*, whereupon this Examinate waxed afraid of her, and was then presently sick, and so pained that shee could not ſtand, and the next day after this Examinate going to Warrington, was suddenly pinched on her Thigh as shee thought, with foure fingers & a Thumbe twice together, and thereupon was sicke, in so much as shee could not get home but on horse-backe, yet soone after shee did mend.

The Examination of M A R G A R E T L Y O N *wife of* THOMAS LYON *the yonger, of Windle aforeſaid: Taken before the ſaid Sir* THOMAS GERRARD, *Knight and Barronet, the day and place a-foreſaid. Againſt the ſaid* ISABEL ROBEY.

THe said *Margaret Lyon* vpon her Oath saith, that vpon a time *Isabel Robey* came into her house and said that *Peter Chaddock* should neuer mend vntill he had asked her forgiuenesse; and that shee knew hee would neuer doe: whereupon this Examinate said, how doe
you

you know that, for he is a true Christian, and hee would
aske all the world forgiuenesse? then the said *Isabel* said,
that is all one, for hee will neuer aske me forgiuenesse,
therefore hee shall neuer mend; And this Examinate
further saith, that shee being in the house of the said *Peter Chaddock*, the wife of the said *Peter*, who is God-
Daughter of the said *Isabel*, and hath in times past vsed
her companie much, did affirme, that the said *Peter* was
now satisfied, that the said *Isabel Robey* was no Witch,
by sending to one *Halseworths*, which they call a wise-
man, and the wife of the said *Peter* then said, to abide
vpon it, I thinke that my Husband will neuer mend
vntill hee haue asked her forgiuenesse, choose him
whether hee will be angrie or pleased, for this is my
opinion : to which he answered, when he did need to
aske her forgiuenesse, he would, but hee thought hee
did not need, for any thing hee knew : and yet this
Examinate further saith, That the said *Peter Chaddock*
had very often told her, that he was very afraid that the
said *Isabel* had done him much hurt; and that he being
fearefull to meete her, he hath turned backe at such time
as he did meet her alone, which the said *Isabel* hath since
then affirmed to be true, saying, that hee the said *Peter*
did turne againe when he met her in the Lane.

The

The Examination of MARGARET

PARRE *wife of* HVGH PARRE *of Windle aforesaid.*
Taken before the said Sir THOMAS GERARD
Knight and Baronet, the day and place aforesaid. Against
the said ISABEL ROBEY.

THE said Examinate vpon her oath saith, that vpon
a time, the said *Isabel Robey* came to her house, and
this Examinate asked her how *Peter Chaddock* did, And
the said *Isabel* answered shee knew not, for shee went
not to see, and then this Examinate asked her how
Iane Wilkinson did, for that she had beene lately sicke and
suspected to haue beene bewitched : then the said *Isabel*
said twice together, I haue bewitched her too : and then
this Examinate said that shee trusted shee could blesse
her selfe from all Witches and defied them ; and then
the said *Isabel* said twice together, would you defie me? &
afterwards the said *Isabel* went away not well pleased.

Here the Gentlemen of the last Iurie of Life and
Death hauing taken great paines, the time being farre
spent, and the number of the Prisoners great, returned
into the Court to deliuer vp their Verdict against them
as followeth. *viz.*

The Verdict of Life and Death.

WHo vpon their Oathes found the said *Isabel Ro-*
bey guiltie of the Fellonie by Witch-craft, contained

tained in the Indictment against her. And *Margaret Pearson* guiltie of the offence by Witch-craft, contained in the Indictment against her.

Whereupon Master *Couell* was commaunded by the Court in the afternoone to bring forth all the Prisoners that stood Conuicted, to receiue their Iudgment of Life and Death.

For his Lordship now intended to proceed to a finall dispatch of the Pleas of the Crowne. And heere endeth the Arraignement and Triall of the Witches at Lancaster.

THus at the length haue we brought to perfection this intended Discouery of Witches, with the Arraignement and Triall of euery one of them in order, by the helpe of Almightie God, and this Reuerend Iudge ; the Lanterne from whom I haue receiued light to direct me in this course to the end. And as in the beginning, I presented vnto their view a Kalender containing the names of all the witches : So now I shall present vnto you in the conclusion and end, such as stand conuicted, and come to the Barre to receiue the iudgement of the Law for their offences, and the proceedings of the Court against such as were acquitted, and found not guiltie : with the religious Exhortation of this Honorable Iudge, as eminent in gifts and graces as in place and preeminence, which I may lawfully affirme without base flattery (the canker of all honest and worthie minds) drew the eyes and reuerend respect of all that great Audience present, to heare their Iudgement, and the end of these proceedings.

The

The Prisoners being brought to the Barre.

THe Court commanded three solemne Proclamations for silence, vntill Iudgement for Life and Death
were giuen.

  Whereupon I presented to his Lordship the
   names of the Prisoners in order, which
    were now to receiue their
     Iudgement.
      ⁂

The

¶ The names of the Prisoners at the
Barre to receiue their Judgement
of Life and Death.

Anne Whittle, alias
Chattox.

Elizabeth Deuice.

James Deuice.

Anne Redferne.

Alice Nutter.

Katherine Hewet.

John Bulcock.

Jane Bulcock.

Alizon Deuice.

Isabel Robey.

THE

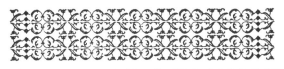

THE IVDGEMENT

OF THE RIGHT HONORABLE

Sir EDVVARD BROMLEY, Knight, one
of his Maiesties Iustices of Assize at Lan-
caster vpon the Witches conuicted,
as followeth.

THere is no man aliue more vnwilling to pronounce this wofull and heauy Iudgement a-
gainst you, then my selfe : and if it were possible, I would to God this cup might passe from
me. But since it is otherwise prouided, that after all proceedings of the Law, there must be a Iudgement;
and the Execution of that Iudgement must succeed and follow in due time : I pray you haue patience to receiue that which
the Law doth lay vpon you.   You of all people haue the least
cause to complaine : since in the Triall of your liues there hath
beene great care and paines taken, and much time spent : and
very few or none of you, but stand conuicted vpon your owne
voluntarie confessions and Examinations, Ex ore proprio :
Few Witnesses examined against you, but such as were present, and parties in your Assemblies. Nay I may further
affirme, What persons of your nature and condition, euer
were Arraigned and Tried with more solemnitie, had more
libertie giuen to pleade or answere to euerie particular point
of Euidence against you ? In conclusion such hath beene the

generall care of all, that had to deale with you, that you haue neither cause to be offended in the proceedings of the Iustices, that first tooke paines in these businesses, nor with the Court that hath had great care to giue nothing in euidence against you, but matter of fact ; Sufficient matter vpon Record, and not to induce or leade the Iurie to finde any one of you guiltie vpon matter of suspition or presumption, nor with the witnesses who haue beene tried, as it were in the fire : Nay, you cannot denie but must confesse what extraordinarie meanes hath beene vsed to make triall of their euidence, and to discouer the least intended practice in any one of them, to touch your liues vniustly.

As you stand simply (your offences and bloudie practlises not considered) your fall would rather moue compassion, then exasperate any man. For whom would not the ruine of so many poore creatures at one time, touch, as in apparance simple, and of little vnderstanding ?

But the bloud of those innocent children, and others his Maiesties Subiects, whom cruelly and barbarously you haue murdered, and cut off, with all the rest of your offences, hath cryed out vnto the Lord against you, and sollicited for satisfaction and reuenge, and that hath brought this heauie iudgement vpon you at this time.

It is therefore now time no longer wilfully to striue, both against the prouidence of God, and the Iustice of the Land : the more you labour to acquit your selues, the more euident and apparant you make your offences to the World. And vnpossible it is that they shall either prosper or continue in this World, or receiue reward in the next, that are stained with so much innocent bloud.

The worst then I wish to you, standing at the Barre conuicted, to receiue your Iudgement, is, Remorse, and true Re-

pentance, for the safegard of your Soules, and after, an humble, penitent, and heartie acknowledgement of your grieuous sinnes and offences committed both againſt GOD *and* Man.

Firſt, yeeld humble and heartie thankes to Almightie GOD *for taking hold of you in your beginning, and making ſlay of your intended bloudie praſtiſes (although* GOD *knowes there is too much done alreadie) which would in time haue caſt so great a weight of Iudgement vpon your Soules.*

Then praise GOD *that it pleased him not to surprize or ſtrike you suddenly, euen in the execution of your bloudie Murthers, and in the middeſt of your wicked praſtiſes, but hath giuen you time, and takes you away by a iudiciall course and triall of the Law.*

Laſt of all, craue pardon of the World, and eſpecially of all such as you haue iuſtly offended, either by tormenting themselues, children, or friends, murder of their kinsfolks, or losse of any their goods.

And for leauing to future times the president of so many barbarous and bloudie murders, with such meetings, praſtiſes, consultations, and meanes to execute reuenge, being the greateſt part of your comfort in all your aſtions, which may inſtruſt others to hold the like course, or fall in the like sort :

It only remaines I pronounce the Iudgement of the Court againſt you by the Kings authoritie, which is ; You shall all goe from hence to the Caſtle, from whence you came ; from thence you shall bee carried to the place of Execution for this Countie : where your bodies shall bee hanged vntill you be dead; And GOD HAVE MERCIE VPON YOVR SOVLES: For your comfort in this world I shall commend a learned and worthie Preacher

to

to inſtruct you, and prepare you for an other World:
All I can doe for you is to pray for your Repentance in
this World, for the satisfaction of many ; And forgiuenesse in the next world, for sauing of your Soules. And
God graunt you may make good vse of the time you
haue in this World, to his glorie and your owne comfort.

Margaret Pearson.

THe Iudgement of the Court againſt you, is, You
shall ſtand vpon the Pillarie in open Market, at *Cli-*
theroe, *Paddiham*, *Whalley*, and *Lancaſter*, foure Market
dayes, with a Paper vpon your head, in great Letters,
declaring your offence, and there you shall confesse
your offence, and after to remaine in Prison for one
yeare without Baile, and after to be bound with good
Suerties, to be of the good behauiour.

To

To the Priſoners found not guiltie
by the Ivries.

Elizabeth Aſtley.
John Ramsden.
Alice Gray.
Isabel Sidegraues.
Lawrence Hay.

T*O you that are found not guiltie, and are by the Law to bee acquited, presume no further of your Innocencie then you haue iuſt cause : for although it pleaſed God out of his Mercie, to ſpare you at this time, yet without queſtion there are amongſt you, that are as deepe in this Action, as any of them that are condemned to die for their offences : The time is now for you to forſake the Deuill : Remember how, and in what sort bee hath dealt with all of you : make good vse of this great mercie and fa- uour : and pray vnto God you fall not againe : For great is your happinesse to haue time in this World, to prepare your selues againſt the day when you shall appeare before the Great Iudge of all.*

Notwithſtanding, the iudgement of the Court, is, You shall all enter Recognizances with good sufficient Suer- ties, to appeare at the next Assizes at Lancaſter, and in the meane time to be of the good behauiour. All I can ſay to you :

X

Iennet

Jennet Bierley,

Ellen Bierley,

Jane Southworth,   is, That G o d
hath deliuered you beyond expectation, I pray G o d
you may vse this mercie and fauour well ; and take heed
you fall not hereafter : And so the Court doth order
you shall be deliuered.

What more can bee written or published of the proceedings of this honorable Court : but to conclude with
the Execution of the Witches, who were executed the
next day following at the common place of Execution,
neare vnto Lancaster. Yet in the end giue mee leaue to
intreate some fauour that haue beene afraid to speake
vntill my worke were finished. If I haue omitted any
thing materiall, or published any thing imperfect, excuse me for that I haue done : It was a worke imposed
vpon me by the Iudges, in respect I was so wel instructed
in euery particular. In hast I haue vndertaken to finish it
in a busie Tearme amongst my other imploiments.
My charge was to publish the proceedings of Iustice,
and matter of Fact, wherein I wanted libertie to write
what I would, and am limited to set forth nothing a-
gainst them, but matter vpon Record, euen in their
owne Countrie tearmes, which may seeme strange. And
this I hope will giue good satisfaction to such as vnder-
stand how to iudge of a businesse of this nature. Such
as haue no other imploiment but to question other
mens Actions, I leaue them to censure what they please,
It is no part of my profession to publish any thing in
                                                    print

print, neither can I paint in extraordinarie tearmes. But if this discouerie may serue for your instruction, I shall thinke my selfe very happie in this Seruice, and so leaue it to your generall censure.

Da veniam Ignoto non displicuisse meretur,
Festinat studijs qui placuisse tibi.

THE ARRAIGNEMENT AND TRIALL OF

IENNET PRESTON, OF
GISBORNE IN CRAVEN,
in the Countie of Yorke.

At the Assises and Generall Gaole-
Deliuerie holden at the Castle of Yorke
in the Countie of Yorke, the xxvij. day of
Iuly laſt paſt, *Anno Regni Regis* IACOBI
*Angliæ, &c. Decimo, & Scotiæ
quadragesimo quinto.*

Before
Sir IAMES ALTHAM *Knight, one*
of the Barons of his Maieſties Court of Exchequer;
and Sir EDVVARD BROMLEY Knight, another of
the Barons of his Maieſties Court of Exchequer;
his Maieſties Iuſtices of Assise, Oyer and Terminer,
*and generall Gaole-Deliuerie, in the Circuit
of the North-parts.*

LONDON,
Printed by W. STANSBY for IOHN BARNES, and
are to be sold at his Shoppe neere Holborne Conduit. 1612.

THE ARRAIGNMENT

and Triall of IENNET PRES-
TON *of Gisborne in Crauen, in the Countie of Yorke, at
the Assises and Generall Gaole-deliuerie, holden at the
Castle of Yorke, in the Countie of Yorke, the seuen and
twentieth day of Iuly last past.* Anno Regni Regis Iacobi Angliæ &c. Decimo & Scotiæ xlvj.

Jennet Preston.

MANY haue vndertaken to write great discourses of Witches and many more dispute and speake of them. And it were not much if as many wrote of them as could write at al, to set forth to the world the particular Rites and Secrets of their vnlawfull Artes, with their infinite and wonderfull practises which many men little feare till they seaze vpon them. As by this late won-
derfull discouerie of Witches in the Countie of Lanca-
ster may appeare, wherein I find such apparant matter to satisfie the World, how dangerous and malitious a
Witch

Witch this *Iennet Preston* was, How vnfit to liue, hauing once so great mercie extended to her : And againe
to reuiue her practises, and returne to her former course
of life ; that I thinke it necessarie not to let the memorie of her life and death die with her ; But to place her
next to her fellowes and to set forth the Arraignement
Triall and Conuiction of her, with her offences for
which she was condemned and executed.

And although shee died for her offence before the
rest, I yet can afford her no better place then in the end
of this Booke in respect the proceedings was in another
Countie ;

You that were husband to this *Iennet Preston* ;
her friends and kinsfolkes, who haue not beene sparing
to deuise so scandalous a slander out of the malice of
your hearts, as that shee was maliciously prosecuted by
Master *Lister* and others ; Her life vniustly taken away
by practise ; and that (euen at the Gallowes where shee
died impenitent and void of all feare or grace) she died
an Innocent woman, because she would confesse nothing : You I say may not hold it strange, though at
this time, being not only moued in conscience, but di-
rected, for example sake, with that which I haue to report of her, I suffer you not to wander any further ; but
with this short discourse oppose your idle conceipts a-
ble to seduce others : And by Charmes of Imputations
and slander, laid vpon the Iustice of the Land, to cleare
her that was iustly condemned and executed for her offence ; That this *Iennet Preston* was for many yeares
well thought of and esteemed by Master *Lister* who
afterwardes died for it Had free accesse to his house,
kind respect and entertainment ; nothing denied her she
stood

stood in need of. Which of you that dwelleth neare them in Crauen but can and will witnesse it ? which might haue incouraged a Woman of any good condition to haue runne a better course.

The fauour and goodnesse of this Gentleman Maﬆer *Liﬆer* now liuing, at his firﬆ entrance after the death of his Father extended towards her, and the reliefe she had at all times, with many other fauours that succeeded from time to time, are so palpable and euident to all men as no man can denie them. These were sufficient motiues to haue perswaded her from the murder of so good a friend.

But such was her execrable Ingratitude, as euen this grace and goodnesse was the cause of his miserable and vntimely death. And euen in the beginning of his greateﬆ fauours extended to her, began shee to worke this mischiefe, according to the course of all Witches.

This *Iennet Preﬆon*, whose Arraignment and Triall, with the particular Euidence againﬆ her I am now to set forth vnto you, one that liued at Gisborne in Crauen, in the Countie of Yorke, neare Maﬆer *Liﬆer* of Weﬆbie, againﬆ whom she practised much mischiefe ; for hauing cut off *Thomas Liﬆer* Esquire, father to this gentleman now liuing, shee reuenged her selfe vpon his sonne: who in short time receiued great losse in his goods and cattell by her meanes.

These things in time did beget suspition, and at the Assizes and Generall Gaole deliuerie holden at the Caﬆle of Yorke in Lent laﬆ paﬆ, before my Lord *Bromley*, shee was Indicted and Arraigned for the murder of a Child of one *Dodg-sonnes*, but by the fauour and mercifull consideration of the Iurie thereof acquited.

Y

But

But this fauour and mercie was no sooner extended towardes her, and shee set at libertie, But shee began to practise the vtter ruine and ouerthrow of the name and bloud of this Gentleman.

And the better to execute her mischiefe and wicked intent, within foure dayes after her deliuerance out of the Castle at Yorke, went to the great Assembly of Witches at *Malking-Tower* vpon Good-friday last: to pray aide and helpe, for the murder of Master *Lister*, in respect he had prosecuted against her at the same Assizes.

Which it pleased God in his mercie to discouer, and in the end, howsoeuer he had blinded her, as he did the King of Ægypt and his Instruments, for the brighter euidence of his own powerfull glory ; Yet by a Iudiciall course and triall of the Law, cut her off, and so deliuered his people from the danger of her Deuilish and wicked practises : which you shall heare against her, at her Arraignement and Triall, which I shall now set forth to you in order as it was performed, with the wonderfull signes and tokens of G o d, to satisfie the Iurie to finde her guiltie of this bloudie murther, committed foure yeares since.

In-

Indictment.

THis *Iennet Preston* being Prisoner in the Castle at Yorke, and indicted, for that shee felloniously had practised, vsed, and exercised diuerse wicked and deuillish Arts, called Witchcrafts, Inchauntments, Charmes, and Sorceries, in and vpon one *Thomas Lister* of Westby in Crauen, in the Countie of Yorke Esquire, and by force of the same Witchcraft felloniously the said *Thomas Lister* had killed, *Contra Pacem &c.* beeing at the Barre, was arraigned.

To this Indictment vpon her Arraignement, shee pleaded not guiltie, and for the Triall of her life put her selfe vpon G o d and her Countrey.

Whereupon my Lord *Altham* commaunded Master Sheriffe of the Countie of Yorke, in open Court to returne a Iurie of sufficient Gentlemen of vnderstanding, to passe betweene our Soueraigne Lord the Kings Maiestie and her, and others the Prisoners, vpon their liues and deaths ; who were afterwards sworne, according to the forme and order of the Court, the prisoner being admitted to her lawfull challenge.

Which being done, and the Prisoner at the Barre to receiue her Tryall, Master *Heyber*, one of his Maiesties Iustices of Peace in the same County, hauing taken great paines in the proceedings against her ; and being best instructed of any man of all the particular points of Euidence against her, humbly prayed, the witnesses hereafter following might be examined against her, and the seuerall Examinations, taken before Master *Nowel*, and certified, might openly bee published against her ; which hereafter follow in order, *viz.*

The

The Euidence for the Kings Maiestie

HEreupon were diuerse Examinations taken and read openly against her, to induce and satisfie the Gentlemen of the Iurie of Life and Death, to finde she was a Witch; and many other circumstances for the death of M. *Lister.* In the end *Anne Robinson* and others were both examined, who vpon their Oathes declared against her, That M. *Lister* lying in great extremitie, vpon his death-bedde, cried out vnto them that stood about him; that *Iennet Preston* was in the house, looke where shee is, take hold of her : for Gods sake shut the doores, and take her, shee cannot escape away. Looke about for her, and lay hold on her, for shee is in the house *:* and so cryed very often in his great paines, to them that came to visit him during his sicknesse.

Anne Robinson,
and
Thomas Lister

Being examined further, they both gaue this in euidence against her, That when Master *Lister* lay vpon his death-bedde, hee cryed out in great extremitie; *Iennet Preston* lyes heauie vpon me, *Prestons* wife lyes heauie vpon me; helpe me, helpe me : and so departed, crying out against her.

                                        These

These, with many other witnesses, were further examined, and deposed, That *Iennet Preston*, the Prisoner at the Barre, being brought to M. *Lister* after hee was dead, & layd out to be wound vp in his winding-sheet, the said *Iennet Preston* comming to touch the dead corpes, they bled fresh bloud presently, in the presence of all that were there present : Which hath euer beene held a great argument to induce a Iurie to hold him guiltie that shall be accused of Murther, and hath seldome, or neuer, fayled in the Tryall.

But these were not alone : for this wicked and bloud-thirstie Witch was no sooner deliuered at the Assises holden at Yorke in Lent last past, being indicted, arraigned, and by the fauor and mercie of the Iurie found not guiltie, for the murther of a Child by Witch-craft : but vpon the Friday following, beeing Good-Friday, shee rode in hast to the great meeting at Malking-Tower, and there prayed aide for the murther of M. *Thomas Lister :* as at large shall appeare, by the seuerall Examinations hereafter following ; sent to these Assises from Master *Nowel* and other his Majesties Iustices of Peace in the Countie of Lancaster, to be giuen in euidence against her, vpon her Triall, *viz.*

The

The Examination and Euidence of

IAMES DEVICE, *of the Forrest of Pendle, in the Countie of Lancaster, Labourer, taken at the house of* IAMES WILSEY, *of the Forrest of Pendle in the Countie of Lancaster, the seuen and twentieth day of* Aprill, *Anno Reg. Regis* IACOBI *Angliæ*, &c. *Decimo ac Scotiæ quadragesimo quinto.*

Before

ROGER NOVVEL, *and* NICHOLAS BANESTER, *Esquires, two of his Maiesties Iustices of the Peace within the Countie of Lancaster, viz.*

THis Examinate saith, That vpon Good-Friday last about twelue of the clocke in the day-time, there dined in this Examinates said mothers house a number of persons, whereof three were men, with this Examinate, and the rest women : and that they met there for these three causes following (as this Examinates said mother told this Examinate) : First was for the naming of the Spirit, which *Alizon Deuice*, now Prisoner at Lancaster, had, but did not name him, because shee was not there. The second cause was for the deliuery of his said Grand-mother, this Examinates said sister *Alizon*, the said *Anne Chattox*, and her daughter *Redferne* : Killing the Gaoler at Lancaster ; and before the next Assizes to blow vp the Castle there ; to that end the aforesaid Prisoners might by that meanes make an escape and get away. All which this Examinate then heard them conferre of. And the third cause was, for that there was a woman dwelling in Gisburne Parish, who came into this Examinates said Grand-mothers house,

house, who there came, and craued assistance of the rest of them that were then there, for the killing of Master *Lister* of Westby : because, as she then said, he had borne malice vnto her, and had thought to haue put her away at the last Assizes at Yorke ; but could not. And then this Examinat heard the said woman say, that her power was not strong enough to doe it her selfe, being now lesse then before-time it had beene.

And he also further saith, That the said *Prestons* wife had a Spirit with her like vnto a white Foale, with a blacke-spot in the forehead. And further, this Examinat saith, That since the said meeting, as aforesaid, this Examinate hath beene brought to the wife of one *Preston* in Gisburne Parish aforesaid, by *Henry Hargreiues* of Gold-shey, to see whether shee was the woman that came a-mongst the said Witches, on the said last Good-Friday, to craue their aide and assistance for the killing of the said Master *Lister* : and hauing had full view of her ; hee this Examinate confesseth, That she was the selfe-same woman which came amongst the said Witches on the said last Good-Friday, for their aide for the killing of the said Master *Lister* ; and that brought the Spirit with her, in the shape of a White Foale, as aforesaid.

And this Examinate further saith, That all the said Witches went out of the said house in their owne shapes and likenesses, and they all, by that they were forth of the doores, were gotten on horse-backe like vn-to Foales, some of one colour, some of another, and *Prestons* wife was the last ; and when she got on horse-backe, they all presently vanished out of this Examinats sight : and before their said parting away, they all ap-pointed to meete at the said *Prestons* wifes house that
day

day twelue-month; at which time the said *Preſtons* wife
promised to make them a great feaſt ; and if they had occasion to meet in the meane time, then should warning
bee giuen that they all should meete vpon Romles-
Moore.   And this Examinate further saith, That at the
said feaſt at Malking-Tower, this Examinat heard them
all giue their consents to put the said Maſter *Thomas Li-*
ſter of Weſtby to death : and after Maſter *Liſter* should
be made away by Witchcraft, then al the said Witches
gaue their consents to ioyne altogether to hancke Maſter *Leonard Liſter*, when he should come to dwell at the
Sowgill, and so put him to death.

The Examination of HENRIE HAR-
GREIVES *of Goldshey-booth, in the Forreſt of*
Pendle, in the Countie of Lancaſter Yeoman, taken the
fifth day of May, *Anno Reg. Regis* IACOBI *Angliæ,*
&c. Decimo, ac Scociæ quadragesimo quinto.

Before
ROGER NOVVEL, NICHOLAS BANNESTER,
and ROBERT HOLDEN, *Esquires ; three of his*
Maieſties Iuſtices of Peace within the said Countie.

THis Examinat vpon his oath saith, That *Anne Whit-*
tle, alias *Chattox*, confessed vnto him, that she knoweth one *Preſtons* wife neere Gisburne, and that the said
Preſtons wife should haue beene at the said feaſt, vpon
the said Good-Friday, and that shee was an ill woman,
and had done Maſter *Liſter* of Weſtby great hurt.

The

The Examination of ELIZABETH

DEVICE, *mother of* IAMES DEVICE, *taken before*
ROGER NOVVEL *and* NICHOLAS BANESTER,
Esquires, the day and yeare aforesaid, viz.

THe said *Elizabeth Deuice* vpon her Examination confesseth, That vpon Good-Friday laſt, there dined at
this Examinats house, which she hath said are Witches,
and doth verily thinke them to be Witches ; and their
names are those whom *Iames Deuice* hath formerly spoken of to be there.

She also confesseth in all things touching the killing
of Maſter *Liſter* of Weſtby, as the said *Iames Deuice* hath
before confessed.

And the said *Elizabeth Deuice* also further saith, That
at the said meeting at Malking-Tower, as aforesaid, the
said *Katherine Hewyt* and *Iohn Bulcock*, with all the reſt
then there, gaue their consents, with the said *Preſtons*
wife, for the killing of the said Maſter *Liſter*. And for
the killing of the said Maſter *Leonard Liſter*, she this Examinate saith in all things, as the said *Iames Deuice* hath
before confessed in his Examination.

Z

The

The Examination of IENNET DE-
VICE, *daughter of* ELIZABETH *late wife of* IOHN
DEVICE, *of the Forreſt of Pendle, in the Countie of Lancaſter, about the age of nine yeares or thereabouts, taken
the day and yeare aboue-said :*

Before
ROGER NOVVEL *and* NICHOLAS BANE-
STER, *Esquires, two of his* Maieſlies Iuſtices of Peace in
the Countie of Lancaſter.

THE said Examinate vpon her Examination saith,
that vpon Good-friday laſt there was about twenty
persons, whereof only two were men, to this Examinats
remembrance, at her said Grand-mothers house, called
Malking-Tower aforesaid, about twelue of the clocke :
all which persons, this Examinates said mother
told her were Witches, and that she knoweth the names of diuers of the said
Witches.

Atter

AFter all these Examinations, Confessions, and Euidence, deliuered in open Court against her, His Lordship commanded the Iurie to obserue the particular circumstances ; first, Master *Lister* in his great extremitie, to complaine hee saw her, and requested them that were by him to lay hold on her.

After he cried out shee lay heauie vpon him, euen at the time of his death.

But the Conclusion is of more consequence then all the rest, that *Iennet Preston* being brought to the dead corps, they bled freshly, And after her deliuerance in Lent, it is proued shee rode vpon a white Foale, and was present in the great assembly at *Malkin Tower* with the Witches, to intreat and pray for aide of them, to kill Master *Lister*, now liuing, for that he had prosequuted against her.

And against these people you may not expect such direct euidence, since all their workes are the workes of darkenesse, no witnesses are present to accuse them, therefore I pray God direct your consciences.

After the Gentlemen of the Iurie of Life and Death had spent the most part of the day, in consideration of the euidence against her, they returned into the Court and deliuered vp their Verdict of Life and Death.

***

The

The *Verdict* of Life and Death.

WHo found *Iennet Preston* guiltie of the fellonie and murder by Witch-craft of *Thomas Lifter*, Esquire; conteyned in the Indictment against her, &c.

Afterwards, according to the course and order of the Lawes, his Lordship pronounced Iudgement against her to bee hanged for her offence. And so the Court a-rose.

HEre was the wonderfull discouerie of this *Iennet Preston*, who for so many yeares had liued at Gisborne in Crauen, neare Master *Lifter* : one thing more I shall adde to all these particular Examinations, and euidence of witnesses, which I saw, and was present in the Court at Lancaster, when it was done at the Assizes holden in August following.

My Lord *Bromley* being very suspicious of the accusation of *Iennet Deuice*, the little Wench, commanded her to looke vpon the Prisoners that were present, and declare which of them were present at *Malkin-Tower*, at the great assembly of Witches vpon Good-Friday last : shee looked vpon and tooke many by the handes, and accused them to be there, and when shee had accused all that were there present, shee told his Lordship there was a Woman that came out of Crauen that was

amongst

amongst the Witches at that Feast, but shee saw her not amongst the Prisoners at the Barre.

What a singular note was this of a Child, amongst many to misse her, that before that time was hanged for her offence, which shee would neuer confesse or declare at her death ? here was present old *Preston* her husband, who then cried out and went away : being fully satisfied his wife had Iustice, and was worthie of death.

To conclude then this present discourse, I heartilie desire you, my louing Friends and Countrie-men, for whose particular instructions this is added to the former of the wonderfull discouerie of Witches in the Countie of Lancaster : And for whose particular satisfaction this is published ; Awake in time, and suffer not your selues to be thus assaulted.

Consider how barbarously this Gentleman hath been dealt withall ; and especially you that hereafter shall passe vpon any Iuries of Life and Death, let not your conniuence, or rather foolish pittie, spare such as these, to exequute farther mischiefe.

Remember that shee was no sooner set at libertie, but shee plotted the ruine and ouerthrow of this Gentleman, and his whole Familie.

Expect not, as this reuerend and learned Iudge saith, such apparent proofe against them, as against others, since all their workes, are the workes of darkenesse: and vnlesse it please Almightie God to raise witnesses to accuse them, who is able to condemne them ?

Forget not the bloud that cries out vnto God for reuenge, bring it not vpon your owne heads.

Neither doe I vrge this any farther, then with this, that I would alwaies intreat you to remember, that it is

as great a crime (as *Salomon* sayth, *Prov.* 17) to condemne the innocent, as to let th˙ guiltie escape free.

Looke not vpon things ſtrangely alledged, but iudici-
ously consider what is juſtly proued againſt them.

And that as well all you that were witnesses, present
at the Arraignement and Triall of her, as all other ſtran-
gers, to whome this Discourse shall come, may take example by this Gentleman to prosecute these hellish
Furies to their end : labor to root them out of the Com-
monwealth, for the common good of your Countrey.
The greateſt mercie extended to them, is soone forgotten.

G o d graunt vs the long and prosperous continuance of these Honorable and Reuerend Iudges, vnder
whose Gouernment we liue in these North parts : for
we may say, that G o d Almightie hath singled them
out, and set them on his Seat, for the defence of Iuſtice.

And for this great deliuerance, let vs all pray to
G o d Almightie, that the memorie of
these worthie Iudges may bee
blessed to all Poſte-
rities.

F I N I S.

The Lancashire Witch-Craze

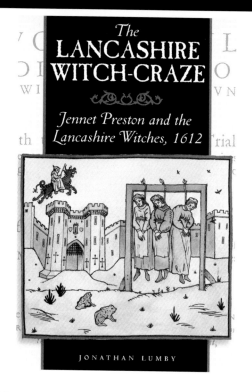

The
LANCASHIRE WITCH-CRAZE

*Jennet Preston and the
Lancashire Witches, 1612*

JONATHAN LUMBY

A remarkable series of new insights are illustrated in this work as the author, Jonathan Lumby, places the events in a wider European context illustrating why these disturbing events occured.

Well-illustrated ISBN 1-85936-065-3 £7.00

The Century Speaks

Recollections of Lancashire Over the Last One Hundred Years

Funny, sad and moving memories of the twentieth century are woven into author Phil Smith's witty, affectionate and lively dialogue and interspersed with many old and new photographs.
An invaluable record.

This fabulous book sold its first print run in just 3 weeks, and is now on to further reprints and still going strong!

ISBN 1-85936-069-6   £10

The First Industrial Society

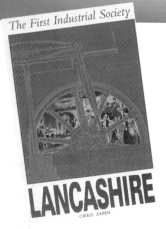

by chris aspin

Covering as it does such varied topics as ballooning, wagering, music, cheap trips, seaside holidays, pleasure gardens and games, as well as the Industrial Revolution itself, this book will entertain all.

Softback, 256 pages, well-illustrated

~~£9.95~~   £6.95

ISBN 1-85936-016-5

The Leeds and Liverpool Canal

The Leeds and Liverpool Canal is England's longest and arguably most successful canal. originally conceived as a way for Bradford merchants to reach the North West port of Liverpool, it was begun in 1770 from both ends simultaneously, and was finally completed in 1816.

The canal runs through near some of the most industrial towns of the North – Liverpool, Wigan, Preston, Blackpool, Burnley, Bradford and Leeds – and for many years carried a large proportion of the goods that fueled the industrial development of the entire region.

Reprinted for 2003

ISBN 1-85936-013-0   £12.00

Cotton Mills in Greater Manchester

Mike Williams with D.A. Farnie

Well-Illustrated
Full colour cover

224 Pages
ISBN 0-948789-89-1

Large-Format
£14.95

Cotton Mills in Preston:
The Power behind the Thread

This unique and invaluable book is the product of the author's passionate interest in the mills which forested Preston's skyline until the latter half of the last century. Colin Dickinson has always been fascinated by the mills, and more specifically the engines which powered them, and without which mass production of cotton would not have been possible.

Many years of meticulous research, supported by visits to mills and interviews with mill workers, has resulted in a book which no-one else could have written in this way. Mill after mill was demolished when King Cotton died, but the author had the foresight to photograph large numbers of them before they disappeared from view. His superb images stand as a permanent record of an industry and way of life that survive only in the memories of the thousands of Preston folk who worked in the mills.

Decade by decade this book charts the role of steam power in the great mills of Preston during the century-and-a-half of their operation. In chronological order it lists every cotton factory to appear on the scene, presenting building dates, site layouts, constructional details, spindleage, loomage, ownerships and final closure dates.

Cotton Mills in Preston: The Power Behind the Thread will enthral those who worked in the mills and is a rich and detailed source of information for anyone interested in cotton mills and steam power.

192 pages   243 x 169   Over 100 unique illustrations
Full colour cover   £12   ISBN

The Roman Frontier in Britain

by david shotter

A fine book about the Roman occupation of Britain and the reasons why they didn't conquer Scotland.

softback, 192 pages, well-illustrated.   £9.95
isbn 1-85936-015-7

Lancashire Gunners At War: 88th Field Regiment, 1939–45
by Stephen Bull

This heroic Lancashire regiment had a hard war. Attacked in the jungle the 88th escaped and went on to see action in Singapore, where they were captured by the Japanese. Nearly half the book covers the experiences of the 88th's survivors in Changi Jail, where they were prisoners until 1945. Here they suffered hunger, maltreatment and over-work as they were forced to build the Burma Railway, including the bridge over the River Kwai. Among the book's many illustrations are paintings by one member of the regiment painted in Changi Jail using brushes made from fellow inmate's hair and paints made using earth and other available pigments. A fascinating and moving account.

160 pages, well illustrated
Full colour cover
Excellent reviews

ISBN 1-85936-068-8   £8.00

Birdwatching Walks in Cumbria

This excellent new book details over fifty gentle walks in Cumbria with excellent birdwatching;

Easy-to-follow route maps are provided for all walks;

Each walk suggests the best places to look, and species to watch out for;

Walks can be planned using the invaluable seasonal occurrence chart which is included;

Written by highly respected and well-known experts in the field.

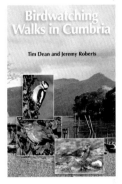

ISBN: 1-85936-074-2 § £7.95 § Available Now §

The Straggling Town

Hilarious Tales of Lancashire Folk

The Straggling Town is set somewhere in `real' Lancashire and will soon make characters like Red Eileen, Bag O' Nails, and Jurassic Jeff household names in the North West and beyond. Using the same combination of humour, wit and poignancy as in *The Century Speaks*, local author Phil Smith has produced another winner, and the stories (many based on real-life incidents) are brilliantly illustrated in cartoons by Matt Wilkins.

192 PAGES, COLOUR COVER, LARGE FORMAT

ISBN 1-85936-079-3 £10

Pub Walks

Duncan's
PUB WALKS
LANCASTER TO THE LAKES

ALL ROYALTIES TO BE DONATED TO CHARITY

What can be better, on a nice day, than walking through the beautiful countryside between Lancaster and the Lake District? Except perhaps a walk that includes a leisurely visit to a pub and then an even more leisurely stroll back to the starting point! Written by avid walker Duncan Turner, each of the 25 excellent walks in this book do just this and are designed for walkers of all ages and abilities. Easy to follow walking instructions are accompanied by useful suggestions, interesting information on the local area, and photographs all of which combine to make this book a must for anyone who enjoys gentle exercise with the option to eat and drink en route.

All royalties from sales of this book will be given by the author to two charities:

Derian House (Charity No. 1005165) is a hospice in Lancashire providing care for terminally ill children, and, like all hospices, it operates without any government funding whatsoever, relying entirely on charitable donations.

Medicine and Chernobyl UK (Charity No. 1039688) (Ribble Valley Branch), is a charity with which the author is involved. Children from Belorus are brought to Britain to get away from the endemic low-level radiation which polluted that country following the Chernobyl disaster. One month's respite during the years of puberty provides children with all they need to recuperate the immune system and give them the strength to live a reasonably healthy life.

160 PAGES, SOFTBACK, HANDY SIZE, EASY TO FOLLOW MAPS & DIRECTIONS, INFORMATION & ILLUSTRATIONS

ISBN 1-85936-083-1   £7.95

SELF-PUBLISHING
WITH CARNEGIE

As you will know, publishers decline to publish manuscripts for many reasons, but in many cases the problem is that the market for them is small and that the writer is neither famous nor well connected. All book publishers will tell you that they have large numbers of manuscripts sitting on their desks, that competition is very fierce and that only books which the publisher feels will sell in high numbers are accepted.

All of which leaves you the author high and dry. But what if you have access to a particular market and know that you can sell a certain number of copies at a certain price, or if you have a group of family and friends to whom you would like to give the special gift of a book you have written, or you need to books quickly for a particular occasion? Perhaps you are willing to fund the production of your book yourself, or can attract sponsorship to cover or contribute towards the costs. So far so good, but where do you go from there?

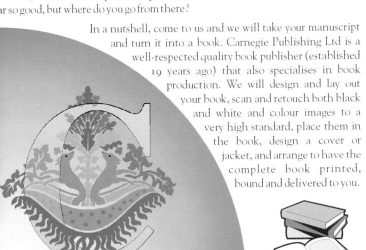

In a nutshell, come to us and we will take your manuscript and turn it into a book. Carnegie Publishing Ltd is a well-respected quality book publisher (established 19 years ago) that also specialises in book production. We will design and lay out your book, scan and retouch both black and white and colour images to a very high standard, place them in the book, design a cover or jacket, and arrange to have the complete book printed, bound and delivered to you.

And because we are book publishers ourselves we can advise you every step of the way on all matters relating to the publication of your own book, including editing, copyright, ISBNs, paper, binding, print runs, retail price (where appropriate), marketing and sales.

So what's the catch? Well there really isn't one. Carnegie Publishing Ltd was established in 1984 and has built a reputation as a producer of high quality books under its own imprint and for other publishers (including well-known academic and public institutions). We can produce books of all types and to fit most budgets and can provide invaluable advice and support for individuals, especially those who have little or no knowledge of publishing books.

Beware of vanity publishers

There is nothing wrong with paying to have your book published, but in our opinion it is very wrong for a publisher to flatter an author about the quality of their book, or to make exaggerated estimates of the potential sales of the book, and especially to charge extortionate prices for the production of books. You may be able to sell sufficient numbers of your book to cover your costs or possibly even make a profit, but in truth it is more likely that you will not be able to do either of these things. Many of the individuals we produce books for just want to experience the pleasure of seeing their work published, and this is a perfectly reasonable aim in itself.

WE CAN GIVE YOU OUR <u>HONEST</u> OPINION AS TO THE QUALITY OF YOUR MANUSCRIPT. WE WILL NOT GIVE YOU FALSE EXPECTATIONS OF THE LIKELY SALES . WE WILL GIVE REALISTIC ADVICE ON THE NUMBER OF COPIES TO PRINT. OUR PRICES ARE FAIR.

If you would like to discuss any of this further, or would like an estimate for the production of your book, just contact Anna Goddard on **01524 840111**. Whether you know a little or a lot about self-publishing, Carnegie can help you to turn your manuscript into books.